ACHIEVING
PERSONAL
EXCELLENCE

Paul Mooney

Published by OAK TREE PRESS, Cork, Ireland

www.oaktreepress.com / www.SuccessStore.com

© 2019 Paul Mooney

A catalogue record of this book is available from the British Library.

ISBN 978 1 78119 364 8 (paperback)

ISBN 978 1 78119 365 5 (ePub)

ISBN 978 1 78119 366 2 (Kindle)

ISBN 978 1 78119 367 9 (PDF)

Cover design: Kieran O'Connor

Cover illustration: © Marko Radunovic / 123rf.com

Illustrations: Ken Lee

All rights reserved. No part of this publication may be reproduced or transmitted in any form or by any means, including photocopying and recording, without written permission of the publisher. Such written permission must also be obtained before any part of this publication is stored in a retrieval system of any nature. Requests for permission should be directed to info@oaktreepress.com.

CONTENTS

Section 3: Brilliant Communications

Section 4: Personal Effectiveness

Section 5: Change Management

FOREWORD

We discovered *Confessions of a Consultant* when it first appeared in 2011 and quickly became fans. The candid viewpoints on personal and organisation development managed to be both witty and thought-provoking. Best of all, the blog offered an easy way to keep up with the latest thinking – while skipping most of the boring 'homework'. With so much competing information from multiple sources, most executives want to 'cut to the chase' in terms of securing the most relevant messages rather than wading through tomes. Paul delivers on that promise in a way that's simple, but never simplistic.

Secure Future: Targeting personal and organisational success, *Confessions of a Consultant* is an excellent fit with our business. Providing independent assurance and advisory services is essentially about securing the trust and financial health of our clients, *today* and *tomorrow*. There's a strong crossover between what we deliver in the marketplace and the central message of the blog. It is possible to continually improve your position when **you** take control of this. Starting as early as possible, even in a modest way, offers the best chance to reach your goals and become financially independent. And, always, you need to ensure that your financial practices are robust – but also cost-effective and efficient.

Our Team: Our vision is simple: to become a trusted, long-term partners to our clients. Through joint collaboration, Vistra Ireland and Simon Shirley Advisors has a team of financial professionals including Chartered Accountants and Qualified Financial Advisors, delivering the highest quality services. Doing business in a fast-changing global environment offers great opportunities, but often comes with a price tag of complexity and ambiguity. Our clients need partners who can bring something different to the table. They want the confidence that we can provide excellent baseline service and expertise. Increasingly, they want unmatched speed to keep up with an ever-changing business landscape. Ultimately, they want solutions that provide a tangible positive impact to their business and financial health – allowing them to move ahead of the game, winning in their respective industries. As leading corporate services providers, we work seamlessly with clients, helping them maximise opportunities.

We've known Paul for many years and are delighted to be involved with the launch of these books. There's so little written about business practices in Ireland that we too often 'import' expertise. So, it's great to see the work of one of our own 'leading thinkers on organisations' sharing his expertise and experience, while adding to his already impressive stock of publications.

Peter Squires
Managing Partner
Vistra

Simon Shirley
Managing Director
Simon Shirley Advisors

INTRODUCTION

Back in 2010, I finished up as President of the National College of Ireland and ventured back into the world of consulting setting up Tandem Consulting. I also started *Confessions of a Consultant* (**tandemconsulting.wordpress.com**), a blog. The idea was to capture and share some of the challenges faced in the world of consulting.

At first, the blogs were occasional – but, quickly, they became more frequent and, in time, weekly. Later, I stepped them back to fortnightly. Surprisingly (to me, at least), the blog achieved over 4,000 subscribers and, based on the feedback I got, by and large it hit the spot for lots of people (in fairness, not everyone is a fan of my quirky sense of humour).

On that basis, I thought it might be interesting to collate the 'best of the best' – especially since I recently stopped updating the blog (although it's still live on **tandemconsulting.wordpress.com**). Brian O'Kane, my long-suffering publisher, was inveigled into reading all the blogs and making the selection for this book and its companion, *Achieving Organisational Excellence*.

Online, each blog included a couple of 'Lighter Notes' at the end – sometimes, on Monday mornings, you'd need a laugh to kick-start your heart. But (rightly or wrongly) we've made a decision not to include the 'jokes' in the book. You've heard them all before anyway!

I hope you enjoy reading this book and find something of value to you in it. Some of the stories are now 'out-of-date' as they were based on events happening at the time – but, hopefully, the core messages are still fully relevant.

Paul

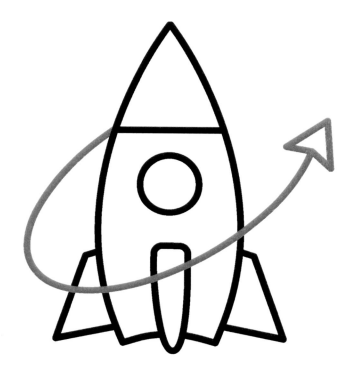

Section 1:

CAREER
DEVELOPMENT

IS IT YOUR AMBITION TO HAVE AN EXTRAORDINARY LIFE?

I couldn't bear to live my life as a normal person.

So said the artist Sean Scully in an interview published in *Cara*, the Aer Lingus inflight magazine. On first glance, the statement seems somewhat arrogant but it raises an intriguing question: Will *you* live an extraordinary life?

And the answer is that most of us don't know what extraordinary looks like.

Lotto Win

For sure, we've all fantasised about coming into a 'chunk of change' or what we'd do with a Lotto win. But, after buying the Porsche, going on a Kruger Park safari and spending a weekend with Cameron Diaz / Brad Pitt (delete as appropriate), what would *you* do next? Most people can't answer, because they have never thought about it.

Planning Permission

Some people believe that life is predestined; forces larger than ourselves guide us along a prescribed route. Others plan in a piecemeal way. They work hard to get promoted, focus on the kid's education or squirrel away money for retirement. But few people ever plan an extraordinary life as a sort of long-term event for themselves. Indeed, the very concept sounds somewhat fanciful. Why?

Undoubtedly, there is a Catholic hang-up about planning for a future that is 'in God's hands'. It's not just an Irish trait. Fears of an 'unknown future' are common across many religions and cultures. The poet Robert Burns expressed it as follows:

> *The best-laid schemes o' mice an' men, gang aft agley (often go awry).*

Granted, we are not entirely in control of our destiny. But does that mean we shouldn't invest any time planning our future?

Bob Fulmer

Professor Bob Fulmer is one of the most interesting guys I ever worked with. At the time, he was a specialist in Organisation Behaviour at Columbia University in New York and had about three 'normal' brains. One day, during a joint presentation, I noticed Bob scribbling furiously at the back of the room. I asked him later how come he was not listening to my brilliant lecture. Turned out he was planning where he and his family would be on New Year's Eve, five years into the future.

I can almost see your reaction. What compulsive disorder was that guy suffering from? Only control freaks make detailed plans five years in advance, right? But, rather than thinking of it as deviant, it's possible to interpret this as planful and goal-oriented behaviour, a human version of the science of cybernetics.

Fulmer later wrote a book about how he planned his retirement when he could choose to live anywhere on the planet (he eventually settled for California).

Full Headlights

So, what can you do with this idea? Well, it depends on whether you see it as being empowered or sort of nuts. If you like the idea, there are loads of possibilities. For example, you could plan your extraordinary life under a number of separate headings:

- Financial independence.
- Positive personal relationships.
- Self-sufficiency in the next generation.
- Relationships with the wider family.
- Work: Staying in your current or another business.
- Philanthropy: Working on the 'give back' agenda.
- Personal time / space.
- Personal and family healthcare.

Too Long?

Perhaps planning for a lifetime seems too long for a first try. How about planning for a perfect year – perhaps:

- Skiing for two weeks in Italy (getting beyond the magic carpet and baby slopes)?
- Golfing for two weeks in the sun?
- Portugal for two months in the winter?
- Travelling across South America for four weeks?
- Spending 20% of your time working in the not-for-profit sector (to save you from going to confession!).
- Family time (working on what *they* want to do).
- Learning to play lead guitar (properly) – maybe Louis Walsh would fix you up in a boy band!

Be Extraordinary

Perhaps the issue that's holding you back is not a lack of control, but squaring up to how powerful you could actually be. Marianne Williamson (in *A Return to Love*) suggested:

> *Our deepest fear is not that we are inadequate. Our deepest fear is that we are powerful beyond measure. It is our light, not our darkness, that most frightens us. We ask ourselves, who am I to be brilliant, gorgeous, talented, fabulous? Actually, who are you not to be? … Your playing small does not serve the world. There is nothing enlightened about shrinking so that other people won't feel insecure around you. … as we let our own light shine, we unconsciously give other people permission to do the same. As we are liberated from our own fear, our presence automatically liberates others.*

Try It

Why not try planning for an extraordinary life? If all else fails, you can always fall back to dating Rosanna Davidson and winning the lottery – *in your dreams.*

But when you focus on being extraordinary, you directly address the question posed by Mary Oliver:

> *Tell me, what is it you plan to do with your one wild and precious life?*

THE SUCCESS RECIPE: WHAT DOES IT LOOK LIKE?

I was dragged out of a deep sleep early last Thursday morning. Cillian had slept through his alarm and was late for work. Daddy Taxi to the rescue - again! The speed limits only apply after 8 am, right? On the way there - dressed in slippers, a dressing gown that's seen better days and the previous night's T-shirt - I was reminded of an innovation I'd seen in New York many moons ago. It was a clock into which you place a $5 (or $50) bill when you set the alarm. If you don't hit the snooze button on time, the phone shreds the note! Genius!

On the way to work, Cillian told me the following story. Last Christmas, his buddy got a present of an alarm clock that physically shoots a projectile to help wake you up. Part of the design is that the missile has to be replaced in its cradle to cut off a piercing air raid alarm siren! One summer morning, when he'd slept with the bedroom window wide open, the missile shot through to the garden below. The guy spent 15 minutes in his jocks (in light Irish summer rainfall), searching for a two-inch plastic missile. Now, *that* would wake you up better than any Americano!

Yes, there's something about getting up early that gets the day off to a flying start. Henry Ward Beecher said:

The first hour is the rudder of the day.

You need to jump up and knock the ice off the rooster!

Success Behaviour

Some people seem to incorporate incredible self-discipline into their lives: getting up early and going to the gym or chairing meetings with the authority of Vladimir Putin. But the rest of us struggle with an energy roller coaster and get distracted by the latest shiny new object (email alerts, the new almond-flavoured Magnum). So, is there some recipe that guarantees success? The ideas listed below seem simple – but they work (most of the time):

- ♦ **Clear goalposts:** Are you clear on what exactly you are trying to achieve and how this will be measured? Today? This week? This year? In his TED talk, Simon Sinek (author of *Start With Why*) makes the point that Martin Luther King didn't become famous for the line: "I have a plan". It was something bigger. So, what's your aim point? What inscription do you want to have engraved on your tombstone? **Aim high**.

- ♦ **Saying "No":** We all need to be loved and want to 'chip in' to resolve life's problems. But for some people this need is so strong, they get run ragged looking for *approval*. You don't have to solve world hunger (every single day). And you shouldn't allow yourself to be bullied by anyone (a boss, aging parent, an overpowering spouse or anyone else). Acquiring the ability to say "No" is a helpful addition to your psychological armoury. **Try assertiveness!** You might like it (and, on the subject of approval-seeking, will all adults please stop posting messages like "Just arrived in Helsinki Airport", unless you need to source a taxi from there). This need for constant attention is not cool and actually damages your brand!

- ♦ **Relinquishing sainthood:** Family therapists tell us that the roles played in early life often continue throughout our entire lives. The first *organisation* we were part of was our family. That's where we learned the rules and how to survive. But, so much of this stuff is unconscious. For example, approval-seeking from a boss (we all do a bit of it) can be likened to looking for attention from a parent. You need to become attuned to the signals. Shy away from conflict? Constantly use humour to lessen tension? Have difficulty in expressing what you really feel? A lot of this stuff has its roots in our nuclear family. In my case, the term 'nuclear' is quite apt. For a couple of years, I unconsciously took up the role of *rescuer*. Like Red Adair, I felt the need to fly around and extinguish all family fires. No more. After a friend, John Randles, said: "Get down off your cross", I soon figured out why I felt compelled to behave like this and was able to discard the fire-fighting uniform. Now, I do stuff I want to do – with a real heart, rather than thinly-disguised resentment. This isn't an argument for selfishness. But it is an argument for **establishing boundaries and sticking to them**. You may not get canonised; but there's a solid chance that you will become *happier* in this life.

- **Self-acceptance:** Who doesn't like James Bond movies? I've always been a little disappointed that those 007 opportunities seemed to pass me by. But, somewhere along the line, I've come to accept myself – flaws n' all. It's taken time (and I'm not fully there yet). But, **if you don't love yourself, it's hard for other people to love you**. Giving up on *perfect* is such a liberating idea, I can't understand why more people don't try it.

- **Shit happens: Part of being resilient means accepting that life is not *fair*** - some good and some bad things will happen. Mike Tyson, the former heavyweight boxing world champion said: "Everyone has a plan until they're punched in the face". I know that this is largely common-sense, but it's not common practice. Some people have a continuing expectation that life will be all powder snow and great skiing – setting themselves up for disappointment. It's like the old cynic's recipe for a happy marriage: set your expectations low!

No doubt you will have your own 'tricks' to keep mentally healthy and positive in the year ahead. Of course, if you are struggling, you can always make a start by purchasing one of those money-shredding alarm clocks. So why not put together your own mental toughness list for the next 12 months?

GETTING AN EDGE: PERSONAL BRANDING

We counted back through the years. The last time we'd been to New York for fun was 1992. Oh sure, I'd made a number of business trips since. But being a 'business hostage' inside some anonymous Ramada Inn basement (sorry, conference room) doesn't count as a life memory.

Plan A

There's always a 'tension' in our family during holidays. In work, I tend to be robotic, working long, planned hours. Then on holidays, my brain automatically reverts to mush and I don't want to think about anything. But Linda insisted. If we didn't put an itinerary together, the week would evaporate and we'd get nothing done. Guess who 'won' that debate? (Again).

Standout Diner

I'd never even heard of Ellen's Stardust Diner. In a city choc-a-bloc with restaurants, what was the point of singling out one in particular? When we got there, a long queue stretched around the corner and the guy on the door estimated the wait as "One hour, buddy". We'd walked past 40 half-empty diners to get here; the kids were starving and cranky; waiting another hour didn't seem like a good idea – even if it was 'on that stupid itinerary'. Despite my protests, wait we did (at one time, I'd suggested that

Linda attend assertiveness classes, but she seems fully cured now!).

Singing Waiters

Oh yes, I forgot to mention that we were told (in advance) that the food in the diner was mediocre. But, it has an edge: the waiters and waitresses are all 'out of work' or wannabe Broadway musical actors. Working off backing tracks, they sang a range of contemporary and classical musical numbers while serving food. Looking directly into Linda's eyes, one particularly good-looking waiter sang the Sam Smyth song *Stay With Me*. I couldn't get her out of the place. The overall show was MC'd by a large guy, who had enough personality for three normal people. Funniest comment: "We're waiting tables and singing our little hearts out. Yes, living the dream". Brilliant.

There are lots of places to eat in New York. But not that many where you queue for an hour in the cold – and say afterwards, "It was worth every minute". In a competitive market, Ellen's Stardust Diner in Manhattan has an edge. **In a competitive business environment, arguably every business needs to have an edge**. Marketers like to call this a USP (unique selling proposition). Turns out that exactly the same point applies to each of us. So, what's *your* USP?

PLOTTING YOUR CAREER SUCCESS: LADDERERS *VERSUS* EXPANDERS

The last time I met Ray Gammell was about three years ago in Abu Dhabi. I was passing through the city on a different mission and called to see him for a chat about Etihad Airways. I've admired Ray for many years and was doubly delighted when he was announced as the interim CEO of the airline, having been promoted from the role of HR Director. Ray demonstrated leadership from his earliest days in the Irish Army, in Intel, Ulster

Bank and, more recently, in the Middle East. It's nice to see the good guys winning (at least, sometimes).

Formal Apprenticeship

Contrast that with a conversation last week with another excellent HR practitioner. A new HR director had been appointed - an internal promotion, but someone from outside the function. My lunch-buddy was making the point that this just wouldn't happen in finance or marketing. His thesis: people 'serve an apprenticeship' within a function and get rewarded by seizing the top spot on the functional ladder at some point. Accountants eventually become financial controllers, then finance directors and so on. But was he correct? Should you stay within your own discipline or jump across and do something else?

Pfizer Leadership

For the past three years, Cathy Buffini and I have been working with the senior engineers across Pfizer globally. There's no 'parish pump politics' at play there. It's definitely not about *who* you know. It's not even about *what* you know. It's all about *what you deliver*. As part of this engagement, we've interviewed a range of senior executives (engineers and others) about their careers - the good, the bad and the ugly. What worked. What didn't. Tripwires that could have been avoided. *Key Point:* So many of the engineers 'crossed over' into other functions (Manufacturing, Quality, HR) that we lost count. And they also moved internationally. In other words, they were *expanders* (moving sideways as parallel opportunities presented) - not *ladderers* (waiting for the next more senior position in engineering to open up). **The route up the corporate mountain is often a zig-zag climb, seldom a straight line**.

Your Career

In thinking about your own career, you might do well to consider the ultimate destination, sometimes referred to as the 'step after next'. Like playing chess, you need to think two or even three moves ahead (in the corporate world, the pieces move around the chessboard surprisingly quickly).

Every year MERC Partners publishes an *Executive Expectations* survey which always makes for interesting reading. In the 2017 survey 59% of executives stated they were much more open to switching roles. People are starting to 'get it'.

One Caveat

But, there's one thing to be mindful of. According to Sir William Osler (a Canadian physician, one of the icons of modern medicine):

> *The best way to take care of tomorrow is to do today's job superbly well.*

Even if your current role is somewhat modest and falls short of being a dream job, you need to over-deliver on this. Career success is the ability to manage a dual-timeframe: planning for *tomorrow* – while making sure that you deliver *today*. My personal belief is that the best time to apply for a job is one year before it's advertised. In other words, **you *apply* for a promotional role, in advance, by delivering a brilliant performance on the job you hold today**.

Alternative Strategy

Of course, you can always pursue an alternative strategy. You can tell your boss:

I'm underperforming in my current role, because it doesn't really suit me. But hey, as soon as I get promoted, I will over-perform in the new (more interesting, more complex, better paid) role.

Good luck with making that sale!

Get Wide

In thinking about the future, don't just see tomorrow as a linear expansion from what you studied or where you are today. Don't allow a study choice you made as a teenager to set boundaries on your life. There's a world of career possibility out there. Go 'wide' and grab it.

MOVING ON:
WHEN'S THE RIGHT TIME TO LEAVE YOUR JOB?

From time to time I meet an executive who's ended up in the wrong job. Sometimes, it's a temporary blip and they just need to sit tight. The chessboard pieces move quickly; if they inhabit a disliked role for 12 or 18 months, it's no big deal over a lifetime career. But, in some cases, the 'misfit' issue runs deeper and punching in more time is not the solution.

Not-for-Profit

I've worked with a range of not-for-profit organisations. For a host of reasons, this sector poses several unique managerial challenges (helping staff to understand that 'not-for-profit' ≠ 'we are for losses' is a useful starting point). In some cases, the CEO is the founder of the organisation. In other cases, s/he is attracted to the sector because they want to 'give something back' to the community. But, being happy in a job requires more than a noble cause. One CEO described this prosaically:

> *Having a great mission doesn't trump all the other shit*
> *I have to put up with.*

The Dilemma

Let's assume that you are a senior executive in a not-for-profit organisation. You are publicly identified with its goals. You've spent a lot of time fundraising, selling the message externally. But you are 'unfulfilled' or secretly have a *grá* for some other line of work. Yet, you've become so identified with the organisation that you feel *stuck*, almost as if your personality and your role have morphed into the same thing.

I am personally aware of two founders of not-for-profit organisations who suffered mental breakdowns as a result of being caught in this specific dilemma (one recently went public in an autobiography that described months when she literally could not get out of bed). They both wanted to move on but felt *trapped*.

Medical Neighbours

Feeling stuck in a rut is not exclusive to not-for-profit organisations. Many years ago, I worked in a medium-sized country town. Living in a new housing development, people made a lot of effort to get to know their neighbours. Three of the guys on the estate were doctors. When we'd meet, two of them would talk about patients, medicine and healthcare. The other invariably would swing the conversation around to computers (his key interest). At some earlier point, that guy, perhaps the brightest boy in his class, got 'pushed' into studying medicine and became a GP because of his own or his family's need to secure a high status occupation. As about 50% of a GP's role is actually counselling, this intelligent but introverted, shy man ended up in a completely unsuitable job with no obvious exit strategy. He should have moved on but felt *trapped*.

Dublin Party

Roll the clock forward 20 years and I'm at a party in Dublin, conducting a 'Bacardi Summit' – solving the problems of the world at 2 am. A woman I'd never met before told me that her partner was hugely committed to a house renovation project in Co. Clare. Restoring its original features had become his life's work. Somewhat envious, I made a range of excuses about why I couldn't do something similar, pleading 'busyness' (forgetting to mention the small matter of a complete absence of DIY skills). Then the lady said: "You don't have your life sorted, do you?" In the cold light of day, that statement seems a smart-assed put-down. But it was simply a question and a solid one at that, one we all need to answer. Do *you* have your life sorted?

The Fear

Many executives worry about leaving an organisation where they've huge service on the clock or have made a significant personal commitment. They ask: "What will happen to the organisation if I move on?" As pushback, I tell them that **the impact of their resignation will be like taking their hand out of a bucket of water and looking to see the space left behind!**

Suit Yourself

When it comes to deciding the best job for you, just suit yourself. Do everyone a favour and chase down a role that you really want. For sure, the announcement that you are *going* will be a five-minute conversation piece, a storm in a thimble. Then people will quickly revert to worrying about their own lives as you get on with yours. All other things being equal (pensions, job security, etc), the right time to leave your job is when you stop enjoying it.

GETTING FIRED:
WHY SOME CAREERS DERAIL

A lot of stuff written about careers is framed in the positive. How to become a great leader. Setting a clear future vision. Bringing staff with you on the journey and so on. But we also know that some people are told to 'walk the plank' – an element of organisation life that is seldom discussed. So, what causes careers to derail? The 'tripwires' detailed below are based on real cases (names and organisation details have been changed to 'protect the guilty'). Here's how it all goes wrong…

Tripwire #1: Rules Only Apply to 'Little People'

Ethical issues will get you fired quicker than anything else. Don't sleep with your PA. Don't accept favours from suppliers. Don't seek personal gain on the company's ticket – because you 'deserve it' (as some sort of payback for those extra hours or weekends you've been working or travelling). Do it and you are dead; it's just a matter of time until someone arranges the funeral.

Unethical and / or fraudulent behaviour accounts for over 40% of the incidences when senior players derail (that's why it's #1 on the list). Like golf, business is a game of ethics. The organisation has to trust you to do the right thing. And ethics is a slippery slope. If it's OK to misstate your expenses on a 'small issue', it soon becomes OK to misstate it on a BIG issue. People get fired for greed – sometimes on quite trivial amounts of money around stuff like RPM (relentless pursuit of mileage). The training unit in Mountjoy prison is not a holiday camp!

Tripwire #2: Missing a Key Performance Target

There is an upper ceiling to the hours you can personally work: 50, 60 or 70, depending on the size of your batteries. During that time, you are in charge of perhaps thousands of hours of outputs. So, **you need to use your time to 'leverage' other people's behaviour**. You need to:

- Know what you personally should be focused on.
- Spend a huge percentage of your time encouraging others to deliver their key outputs.

Now, unless you're an airline pilot, I'm guessing that 'miles flown' is not a strategic measure of your success. Stop telling people how busy you are and get focused on what you need to produce (telling people how busy you are is based on an underlying need for approval: "Look at me. I'm important. Just saying, in case you didn't notice"). Don't get caught up in the classic confusion between inputs and outputs. Focus on what you are trying to accomplish. Like Brazil, it's not a defence to say, "We lost the game 7-1 to Germany, but we made a lot of excellent passes" (anyway, I've seen better 'passes' made on Copacabana Beach).

Tripwire #3: Failure to Build a Top-Class Team

You understand the need to be future-focused, overcoming today's problems while building for the future. You don't just work *in* the business, but also *on* the business. Right?

In some organisations, you may not get 'called' on this – because the culture is relatively short-term-focused and the institutional memory is on par with a hamster's – every 20 seconds is a new day. But **the best-managed organisations look to their managers to build solid leadership teams that represent future capacity and growth potential**. An inability to build and lead a team is an important derailment factor, mentioned in about one out of four of the cases in the literature.

One explanation for this may be that traits like assertiveness and personal initiative get managers onto the fast track in the early part of their careers. Those traits, which make you look like a hero when working as a solo contributor, later get in the way as executives face the challenge of employing a more participative approach. Some people fail to learn this 'new' stuff and it gets them into trouble later in their careers. You are not alone!

Tripwire #4: Confusing Intelligence with Leadership

This one translates as follows: I'm clever, therefore I lead. Usually, to get into senior roles, a person is smart, sometimes incredibly smart. They demonstrate competence in earlier roles and get promoted on the back of this. But 'smartness' (measured by a high IQ) is a very different characteristic than the ability to lead people (usually measured by a high IQ, coupled with a high EQ). In short, being smart and leadership ability are two completely different competencies. Just because you are a world-class snooker player doesn't automatically mean that you can swim.

And **don't forget the role that politics plays in all organisations**. When things go wrong, you need 'credits in the bank' to tide you over. I'm not suggesting that you deliberately go out of your way to keep everyone happy as some sort of 'insurance policy' against future mistakes, but there is an element of personal marketing in all successful careers (unless you find oil in your back garden). People with poor interpersonal relationships, typically don't have 'credits'. "I don't do politics" is often code for "I don't have the skills to understand how politics works".

Example: Cultural arrogance – that is, MY country is better than yours! Here's a simple recipe for 'screwing up'. Take an executive from a 'first world' economy and send them to a developing country. Then watch carefully as the new manager begins to *compare* (that's code for 'rate as inferior') every single thing in the developing country *versus* her / his home country. People from some cultures 'transplant' better than others. Some are almost chameleon-like and take on the identity and the cultural mores of the place they move to. Others don't. They rail against difference. They compare everything negatively. They play a stupid game called 'I wish it was more like home'. And they ultimately fail in their quest to *change the culture of the place where they live into the culture of the place where they have come from.* Sometimes highly-intelligent people can be very stupid.

Tripwire #5: Stopping Learning: Everything I Need to Know, I Already Know

You have a wall plastered with degrees and certificates, some from prestigious institutions. You have a track record of success. You've made a lot of money. People LISTEN when you speak. It's all good. Until you encounter something new, something where you don't fully understand the rules. For example, when an executive moves into a new industry, there is a ton of learning to be done; some of this information is 'tacit' and not easily picked up. It creates a high degree of discomfort.

There's a concept in psychology called dissonance. Most people experience this when they come up against contradictory information or stuff they just don't understand. It's a form of confusion, even mental pain. One way to overcome dissonance is to make a quick decision that gets rid of the confusion. *Example:*

"OK, things are a bit different, but it's all surface stuff. Fundamentally, everything is the same. The best way to manage in the NEW environment is to continue to manage the way I did in the OLD environment". *Voilà!* The dissonance disappears. You have a strategy. That's the good news. The bad news is that you might be headed 180 degrees in the wrong direction. Oops!

You can only overcome this by staying open to learning – and learning to live with the discomfort of 'not knowing everything'. **When the only criteria you use is speed, be careful you don't just get to the wrong place faster**.

Tripwire #6: Inability to Change Despite Feedback

The final tripwire revolves around an executive's ability to adapt to changes required during personal and organisational transitions. It can have several dimensions, including a failure to adapt to a new boss with a different style, overdependence on a single skill or an inability to adapt to the demands of a changing market. Stand still and die! Are you really hearing what your boss is saying? How do your 360-degree results stack up against peer groups? Soon-to-become derailed managers are often unable or unwilling to learn from feedback.

They say: "Yes, that's true but…" (then go on to show they don't believe it's true).

They say: "That's really useful, the most direct feedback I've ever received" (but do absolutely nothing to respond, indicating that it wasn't actually useful).

They say: "It's a lot to take on board. Can you give me a bit of time?" (as a way to end an uncomfortable session and then subsequently ignore the feedback).

Essentially, some people are immune to change. **All senior executives have to be willing to work on tough personal developmental issues**, taking an in-depth look at self-esteem, their ability to deal with new and ambiguous situations and letting go of personal achievement in favour of team-empowerment. The learning involved can be highly emotional and demands an elevated level of maturity.

Conclusion

Most organisations don't take a benign view of managerial underperformance. Once a position is accepted, the executive is expected to perform. Very few transfer back to the starting line with the organisation taking the 'hit' for a poor judgment call.

Moving up in an organisation is usually a one-way ticket. Follow the simple rules outlined above to make sure that you're ready for the journey.

DROWNING EXECUTIVES: ARE YOU OUT OF YOUR DEPTH?

The author of *The Peter Principle*, Lawrence J Peters, coined the memorable phrase:

> *Everyone gets promoted to their level of incompetence.*

Many of you will have worked for managers who've proven the concept! Recognising underperforming executives is not just a menu item for canteen cynics. It's a very real phenomenon that has to be recognised and dealt with. Because all organisations, commercial and not-for-profit, public and private sector, need solid leadership.

Sometimes – not too often – Tandem Consulting is asked to work with an organisation trying to fire someone, typically a senior executive. The person may have performed well at some point and then *fallen off the ladder*. Or they may have been a poor hire – a square peg to begin with, someone who never fit the particular job. Always we try to manage the process with some dignity for the individual (while it's difficult to be fired in a *dignified* way, there are a myriad of undignified ways to do it).

Establish Baselines

The first (diagnostic) step is to establish the baseline. How long is the person in the role? What key skills are required? What positive elements of performance have been demonstrated in the past?

Where are the measurable performance gaps? What conversations have been held directly about the presenting issues and did it produce any change? Does the person accept the performance deficit or are they in denial? The $64,000 question: Is this 'fixable'?

Sadly, it's sometimes the case that the person is the last to know about their underperformance. Senior executives are notorious about shying away from giving feedback – particularly where this is negative. So the person involved often does not see it coming and is typically shocked by the speed of the process. Once this particular train leaves the station, it's hard to stop the forward momentum. Despite a raft of protective legislation, this is a David *versus* Goliath battle – in which the employee normally loses. So, here's the real trick. Don't try to mount a solid defence; avoid getting into this position in the first place.

Managing Perception

Sometimes, actual performance becomes confused with perceived performance. Perhaps you've forgotten to 'tell the world how great you are'. You could take a leaf out of Marketing 101 as suggested by Lord Leverhulme, the founder of Lever Brothers, who said:

> *When you whisper down a well,*
> *About the goods you have to sell,*
> *You'll never make as many dollars*
> *As he who climbs a tree and hollers.*

Anticipating Danger

Let's assume that you are good on the internal marketing front and have covered off on it. How can you determine whether you are still swimming out of your depth? The following checklist identifies the usual warning signs. Go on, take the test. You know you want to!

Am I Out of My Depth?

- ♦ Informal feedback has signalled 'some concerns'.
- ♦ You have recently missed key deadlines.
- ♦ Your performance rating has slipped this year.
- ♦ Your bonus has been frozen.
- ♦ The customer defection rate is heading north.
- ♦ You sometimes lose sleep thinking about work.
- ♦ Peers stop talking when you enter a room.
- ♦ You feel tired a lot of the time.
- ♦ You don't get invited to lunch.
- ♦ You hate Sundays (thinking about work).
- ♦ You constantly moan about your boss.
- ♦ You question the organisation's values.

Sharp Antennae

If you can answer "Yes" to four or more of the above statements, it might be time to buy a copy of *What Color is My Parachute?* and sharpen that CV. Or take a step sideways (or backwards) and re-enter your competency zone. Maybe even try something completely new and refresh. There is no 'do nothing' option.

Personal CEO

Whatever you decide to do, don't just blunder off the edge of the cliff. **You are the CEO of your own life**. Secure the future by doing today's job superbly well. Alternatively, get out there and create something completely new. Either as a great employee or as a self-employed *wunderkind*, you have both hands firmly on the steering wheel of your own career. The key is to be proactive. In the immortal words of Captain Furillo of *Hill Street Blues* fame:

Let's do it to them before they do it to us.

Then the only time you will ever hear the phrase "You're fired" is watching *The Apprentice* on TV. Sleep tight!

GET THE JOB YOU WANT

A question for you: **Are you fishing where the fish are swimming?**

I recently worked with a CEO, helping her to land a new job. She put huge effort into the process and it all worked out in the end. So, what's the BIG deal? Well, in my experience, this high level of effort is the exception rather than the norm. I never cease to be amazed at how clever people can be really stupid when it comes to preparing (in reality, not preparing) for job moves. Some people put more effort into planning a date than their career. So, if getting a new job is on the agenda for you in the coming year, here's a few 'tricks of the trade' to consider.

- ♦ **Brilliant CV:** This seems like a 'baby point' – hardly worth mentioning. But some people pay little attention to this key document. Your CV needs to be *outcomes-based*: what you have achieved – not what you were responsible for. It needs to be geared towards the *particular position* (you need to know what the actual job requires rather than relying on a standard pitch). And it needs to be *truthful*. Don't spoof; truth is just a click away. It needs to be two pages maximum, with language and layout that's punchy and attractive. It needs to make the reader scream: "I want to meet this person". Think about creating a multi-media CV with clips from promotional work you've done or even a one-minute video interview of yourself. Does your current CV pass the 'brilliant' test? As a by-the-way, a survey of 2,200 hiring managers (by CareerBuilder) highlighted the term 'best of breed" as the single most irritating description people used to describe themselves. Don't use it. You have been warned!

♦ **Investigative homework:** You'd be amazed at how many people just 'show up and see what happens' at an interview. They know very little about the products, turnover, structure or the organisation culture. They don't know who they will be meeting, what their biases are or how this position came into being. They are children interviewing for an adult's job. And when the 'Dear John' letter arrives, they blame the process and rationalise their own failure (*"I heard absolutely nothing for five weeks. Who'd want to work for them anyway?"*). Too busy to do this level of homework? Then pay someone else to do it for you (or just get ready to accept a 'long service' award from your current employer).

♦ **Practice interviews:** You will probably only get about four really good jobs in a career lifetime. So, you have to make sure that when the right opportunity comes up, you nail it. And guess what? Practice makes perfect –whether you're playing the violin or getting ready for a CEO interview. Grab your favourite headhunter and ask for a full-blown interview (not a 'chat' over coffee about interviews in general but a mock interview for the actual role you are applying for). When you've taken the feedback on board and sharpened up, you should then assemble a panel of people whom you know / respect and do it all over again. Ask them to be brutally honest. Then go away, lick your wounds and sharpen up. Steal the SAS's motto: "Train hard, fight easy". If you get to this point, the interview will be a doddle! Oh yes, I know that you are also too busy to do this. All those emails to be answered today. It's a killer, isn't it? Not preparing for interviews is a career killer – even if you are 'great on your feet'.

- **Higher IQ:** You can improve your IQ score *by about 10 points* through practice. Go into Eason's or the local library or get on-line and buy or borrow a 'Test your IQ' book. Then practice the exercises. Like getting into the groove on crossword puzzles, you get better at this stuff. A good bit better. It's match fitness. Regardless of whether you are asked to play rugby or go swimming, you are getting mentally ready for the big event. My working assumption is that you're already smart. The trick is to make yourself *smarter* and get the edge over the person who will come second (otherwise known as 'the loser').

- **Cover tracks:** The most recent statistics suggest that 48% of people check Facebook first thing each day (28% check before they get out of bed). There 2+ million members in Ireland who spend 7X more time on it than on any other website. Great if you like spending time on Facebook. Awful if you've posted your drunken escapades under the heading of 'wasted'. Think about the jobs you will be applying for 10 years from now and don't put anything stupid on this or any other social media site. In the criminal investigation world, the motto is: 'Every contact leaves a trace'. It works the same on social media. If you are not IT-literate, phone a friend and get this done for you.

- **The interview:** This one is easy. Look the part. Strong handshake, warm smile. Answer the questions directly (based on the answers that you had prepared in advance, of course). Tell the truth and be positive. And, like a politician, know the points you want to make in advance and make them – regardless of what questions are asked. The interview itself is a walk in the park when all the 'prep' has been done – provided you don't have an 'interview routine' that focuses on *"28 things I'm good at"*. Less is more. How about three things and one thing you are working on / developing. Interviewers are often bored. Don't add to that.

When there are 'no bites today', sometimes fishermen don't mind. They enjoy the process as much as the outcome. But people searching for a job seldom love the process. It's all about the outcome. With few senior roles on offer, you need to ensure that your marketing efforts are successful. This year, move onto that bigger and better pitch. Go on, reel it in!

Section 2:

MENTAL RESILIENCE

CHANGING PEOPLE'S
EXPECTATIONS OF YOU

Like most men, I get fed up shaving. Every single day, sometimes twice a day, the unending ritual continues. Shaving requires all the gear. Cream, a sharp razor, loads of hot water and aftershave. So this year, on holidays, I stopped. Grew a beard for three weeks. Although it didn't make me look even remotely like George Clooney, I enjoyed the freedom from routine and the new image.

Not everyone was a fan. The reaction at home (Linda and the kids) was to remind me of the three phases of man. First, you believe in Santa; second, you become Santa; third, you look like Santa. After 11,423 negative comments, I caved in and shaved it off.

Changing Behaviours

People who work in the addiction area highlight that one of the difficulties in getting clients to quit (drinking, taking drugs or whatever) is to overcome the negative reaction from partners and family. Members of a family take a stance in relation to the addict (typically, either support or critique roles). If the person with the addiction changes their behaviour, this can 'upset the pattern' and subtle pressure (often unconscious) is put on the addict to go back to their normal routine. It seems weird, even counter-intuitive, but patterns of expected behaviour become established and 'roles' develop around this. These roles are stable over time and can be difficult to shift, even where the shift is towards something more positive. No man is an island; **making sustainable behavioural changes impacts both the client and also the key people they interact with**. Why? Because if *I* change, it impacts *you*.

Overcoming Resistance

In coaching executives, I have encountered 'resistance to change' many times. If the person being changed exhibits resistance, it is usually easy to spot – and a range of tactics to recognise and confront resistance are part of the coach's standard 'toolkit'. But when resistance to change comes from people whom the executive coach never meets, then the client needs to be skilled up to recognise and deal with this subtle sabotage. They need to expect resistance and be helped to understand and overcome it.

Push Back

Take an example where an executive is 'overly strong' and makes all judgment calls. Based on negative feedback or personal reflection, the executive decides to change to a more democratic, inclusive style of management. Paradoxically, when they attempt this, the feedback from the senior team may be that they have become 'wishy-washy' or lack interest / personal conviction in the business. The self-same executives, who complained about the leader's authoritarianism, may now take the exact opposite stance. By changing his / her behaviour, the leader has put pressure on others to do the same. Because when *I* change, it impacts *you*.

Going Public

It takes time for new behaviours to be recognised as a style (not simply an aberration) and for people around the executive to change their own roles. In the example above, the expectation may be that the senior team will become more actively involved in decision-making. Where the role of 'moaning' about the leader's behaviour has been made redundant (because the leader has actually changed), other executives sometimes scramble to discover a new role that dovetails with this. So, how can this be progressed?

Sometimes I advise executives to announce that they will be doing something different (working from home on Tuesdays, entertaining key customers, not proof-reading the board information pack, etc.). Making a public pronouncement that they will be different (provided it's been well-thought-out in advance) can help to make their new behaviour understandable and eliminate any efforts to reverse it. A *caveat* is that some things cannot be openly communicated ("OK everyone, listen up. I am not going to get pissed at lunchtime in the future, except on Fridays") and will need to be walked rather than talked.

Changing Expectations

Changing behaviour is difficult. Not alone do you have to break your own patterns, but you may also have to re-programme the expectations of others that you will continue to behave as you have done previously. **Changing people's expectations of you is a potentially useful weapon in your ambition to create a new and improved version of yourself**.

So, this is an advance warning to my own gang. Next year, I'm going for the full four-week beard. Maybe I will even keep growing it, post-holidays. And I don't care if the kids tell me to apply to Arnotts for the Christmas season. So that's that. Sorted!

WHAT DO THE 'BEST' MANAGERS DO?

I was recently asked to make a presentation to an executive team at a Dublin hotel. They wanted a quick recap on what the 'best' managers do. The presentation had to be "15 minutes or less".

While most of us know this stuff already – the key is putting it into practice. **If you were on trial for being a great manager – based on the following checklist – would there be enough evidence to convict you?**

Allocate Time

Most of us have two elements to our role. We have a *specialist* element – client servicing or engineering – and a 'management' piece – helping the people who report to us to service clients or complete engineering projects. The trick here is to avoid the gravitation pull into *doing* (which is often more personally *satisfying* than managing).

To make sure that you are investing sufficient time in managing, you need to diary it. This can be both formal (planned 'Monday Meetings') and informal (walkabouts). Superquinn issued badges to managers with the tagline YCDBSOYA (You can't do business sitting on your arse). *Key Point:* Every manager decides *how* to do this; but they shouldn't decide *if* it gets done or not. **There are no spectators on the managerial pitch**. It's part of the set menu. If you don't have an appetite for this, why not get another job?

Leverage Performance

What percentage of your personal ability is being used in the job? Not just long hours, but your real potential? Now ask that same question of everyone who works for you. The managerial job is to get 'all the troops' into fifth gear – turbo-charged teams of staff. This doesn't somehow magically happen. On a collective basis, people need to know that they are working for an organisation that *stands for* something. They need to have *challenge* in their role. The *goalposts* need to be clear. They (and you) should use feedback as the game progresses – don't wait till the final whistle to figure out the score.

Managing is an unselfish task. It's about *them,* not *you*. Give up your Red Adair complex (wanting to put out all the fires yourself) and let others don the firefighter's suit. It's amazing what you can achieve when you don't need to take credit for it.

Great Communication

Great communications isn't a question of becoming a raving extrovert. We all have our own style (which is pretty difficult to change – for example, there was a lot of consulting money spent on Hillary). It's about three things:

- ♦ Setting up a system to do this – see *Leverage Performance* above.
- ♦ Becoming a great listener – a much underrated communications skill where introverts have a head start.
- ♦ Overcoming the cardinal sin of communication – being boring! Taking a few risks around how you deliver messages can really pay off.

But, ultimately, **great communication is not about *tricks*. It's about sincerity** – a sincere wish to improve your own and others' performance.

Embrace Conflict

Most of us have a hardwired need to be liked – it's part of the human condition (sociopaths can skip this section). That's great, provided… it doesn't get in the way of managing. Being a manager inevitably pushes you up against tough decisions. Underperformance is an obvious example. Feedback is like a 'growth hormone' for people (when it's handled well – and is constructive rather than destructive). **You have to learn to give both positive and developmental feedback, even when this is personally uncomfortable**. The good news is that it gets easier as you practice.

Sometimes the best ideas are simple. But, don't confuse simple with simplistic. 2+2 = 4: the math is simple. It's also correct. This stuff delivers. So should you!

JUST GET IT DONE! EXCUSES DON'T COUNT FOR CEOs

My first HR job was with General Electric. I was on the lowest rung of the managerial ladder and keen to observe how 'managers behaved'. Prior to developing your own style, you mimic the style of others and I was a magpie for stealing ideas (it has become a lifelong trait).

The Sands Hotel

We had an off-site meeting in the Sands Hotel (no, not Las Vegas, Sands in Portmarnock) to review the set-up plans for the manufacturing plant. The general manager, John Donnolly, was a genial American. However, his laid-back style masked an inner steel core. One of the supervisors in the group was relaying the 'Five Sorrowful Mysteries' – a litany of reasons for something that had not been completed on time. Donnelly's riposte was sharp: "I took a Master's degree in excuses. And, guess what? None of them ever got the job done". The supervisor left the company a short time later. He was unhappy with GE and the company was unhappy with him: a marriage made in hell.

Steve Jobs

In an article in *Fortune* magazine (*How America's hottest – and most secretive – big company really works*), Steve Jobs made a very similar point. Apple then had a turnover of $100 billion a year and a growth rate of about 60%. So, how does a behemoth company behave like a start-up?

One of the lessons that Jobs taught all new VPs he called the 'Difference between the Janitor and the Vice President'. If the garbage is not emptied and he asks the janitor "Why?", he might get an excuse like "The locks have been changed and I don't have a key". The janitor gets to explain why something went wrong. VPs don't. Somewhere between the janitor and the senior executive level, reasons cease to matter. **You said you'd do it; you didn't; you're fired**.

Tough?

Yes, for sure, it is tough. But tough goes with the territory. Look at the levels of underperformance we've seen in corporate Ireland in recent years. And how many people were fired? Everyone wants the *package* of a senior executive but the *tolerance* that would be extended to a janitor. You can't have it both ways.

Company boards need to apply the 'logic of senior executive performance' to the people they manage. For sure, individuals can hit speed bumps. External events conspire against them or they have to overcome difficult personal issues. I'm not suggesting that, at the first performance blip, executives should get dragged around the back of the factory and shot. But, if it walks like a duck and quacks like a duck… If you want to protect your job and your income, just get it done!

YOU'RE IN SALES:
GET OVER IT!

Twenty years ago, as a young consultant with jet brown hair, I sat opposite a potential client in a large bank. I'd listened attentively as he described the organisation culture in detail. He chronicled the issues along with his 'personal GPS', how he intended to get through the maze of problems faced. Then, he asked: "Well, what exactly are you selling?" I was somewhat taken aback. I didn't really see myself as 'selling' anything – at least not something that was pre-packaged and ready-to-eat. If the truth be told, I had an in-built snobbery that consulting was somehow 'above' selling. I've since witnessed exactly the same response with CEOs of not-for-profit organisations who almost resent being questioned by potential funders about their organisation or its achievements.

In the bank case detailed, I muttered some stupid made-up answer about developing customised solutions. You could almost see the shutters dropping down over the potential client's eyes. Guess what? I didn't get the job. *Lesson learned:* It's up to me to tell the client what I can do, not up to the client to uncover my 'greatness'.

Last Week

It happened again last week. At the end of a long briefing, a potential client said: "So, what is it that you are insanely good at?"

He followed almost immediately with **"What are the three jobs that you are most proud of?"**

Despite the earlier 'lesson', I still didn't have a great ready-made answer. I'd like to think that this partly indicates humility; I don't like people who boast about their achievements and I try not to be too smug. But, in sharp contrast and much more arrogantly, I *felt like* saying "Did you check my CV / LinkedIn profile / read my stuff" – as if *he* needed to do more homework! Wow! In a single mental step, I'd managed to outsource the blame. My lack of marketing skills was somehow the client's fault!

What happened? He never phoned, he never wrote.

Hard to Describe

The job of an Organisation Development consultant has always been difficult to describe with precision. When people ask me what I do, 10 minutes later they stumble away, bored and still confused. Sometimes, if I'm not going to meet the person again (for example, someone sitting in the next seat on an airplane), I might even chance a 'white lie' and say, "Management trainer" or something that's easy to grasp (perhaps "Recovering academic"?). Of course, I could say that I have good judgment or tell people that I'm in the business of 'fog clearance'. But, faced with a vague answer like that, they are likely to run out the door or have me mentally certified rather than wish to extend the conversation.

Be Clear

Here's the rule: If you are confused about what you do, others will also be confused. Get yourself a 'killer pitch'. Then, grow up and start to use it. We're all in Sales. Get over it.

LEADERSHIP: ARE YOU UP TO THE MARK?

I was recently hired to facilitate a conference on executive development for high-potential engineers, who were smart and good fun. At the end of three days, we came up with nine Leadership commandments. How many of these can you apply in your job?

- **Definition:** Leadership = *the ability to bring about positive change.* Change does not belong to any specific personality type. Introverts can make things happen too! It's not about 'look at me'! It is about 'look at what I've achieved'.

- **Managers manage 'today':** Leadership is focused on *tomorrow.* While it's never 100% tomorrow, if you are 100% focused on today you're not leading, you are managing. The real 'trick' is to learn to manage both timeframes – at the same time (you won't get away with completely ignoring today stuff).

- **Future vision:** How do you determine what 'tomorrow' will look like? To create *tomorrow*, you can demonstrate your individual genius, *or* you can ask for help. You are surrounded by genius. Customers, suppliers, competitors, staff. People are 'oil gushers' of creativity. All for free. Get on that train or plane. But… you can only do this if you create 'space' in your diary.

- **Share the news:** Once you've assembled the data, your job then becomes 'Director of Fog Clearance'. Creating 'certainty' for the people who work for you has to be managed alongside being able to personally tolerate ambiguity (by implication, tomorrow is never 'certain'). The trick is to build personal tolerance for not knowing the answer to everything – you essentially become 'comfortable being uncomfortable'.

- **But, I'm so busy:** You need to create space in your diary to work on the 'tomorrow agenda'. How? Two tools: delegation and rigorous time management. We all have the same number of hours. Being busy is OK as an excuse at a moment in time – but not as a lifelong 'get out of jail' card – an excuse or explanation for *never* moving the needle forward (in the leadership game, marginal movements don't count).

- **Little old me:** You can really make a difference – both with individuals and with full teams. Paddy Kelly, the property developer, started his working life as carpenter. Somewhere along the way, he locked onto the following idea: "If it has to be, it's up to me". How much ambition do you have for your area? Where is your real passion? Can you 'serve a new apprenticeship' in leadership? Can leading become your trump card (over and above your core discipline)? It can be a bit scary to 'take a stand' or deliver bad news. It's scary to swim against the consensus. All the attention is paid to the athlete who 'has the ball'. Take small steps. Learn to lead incrementally. But do it now. Don't be a leader 'tomorrow'. Start being a leader today (by bringing about positive change).

- **Don't rush it:** Oops! Try to avoid the usual 'tripwires' – look at the New Manager Assimilation Program (on the Tandem Consulting website). Don't be arrogant on Day 1.

Listen hard. Take time to understand. Then make changes. Leadership is not measured with a stopwatch.

- **Storytelling:** As the world becomes more 'digital-friendly', multi-media can be very powerful (and sometimes great fun). But... 'old technology' (for example, storytelling) works well too. It's not either / or: use both. Being graphic (in words and pictures) helps messages to stick. And, it's seldom a one-off; you have to *campaign* change programmes – sometimes using marketing / advertising techniques ('If Carlsberg did leadership...').

- **Be positive:** All successful leaders are positive. They find ways 'around roadblocks'. This is not the same as 'saluting the company flag' on the launch of every single new initiative. You are not Pollyanna. While no organisation allows 'internal opposition', you have to be true to yourself and not falsely positive all the time. In the final analysis, leaders are 'real' – ordinary people who manage to create extra-ordinary results by focusing and leveraging the talents of people around them. While we might never become Nelson Mandela or Mother Teresa, we can become the very best that we can be. That's the lifelong challenge for all of us.

WHY DO SMART PEOPLE DO STUPID THINGS?

I think it was the English journalist Francis Wren who said that the world was becoming monopolised by *'process morons with Blackberries and iPhones'*. His central point was that **the *process* (the way we do things) has obscured the *purpose* (the why we do things)**.

Institutionalised Stupidity

He might be onto something. I discovered this when undergoing a minor medical procedure in the Mater Public Hospital. Late one night, a nurse woke me up to give me a sleeping pill. You couldn't make it up. However, the really interesting organisation question is *"Why do clever people do stupid things?"* And, the answer is (usually)… because that's the way it's always been done. Processes in organisations play the equivalent role to tracks in Irish Rail. Everything moves along the existing path – and few people even question this. The best employees 'move faster' along the existing tracks. They are programmed to deliver, rather than to ask the potential breakthrough question: *"Should we be doing this at all?"* Yet, in many organisations the best way forward is not to superglue existing inefficiencies, but to tear up the blueprint and start again from scratch. It's a road seldom travelled.

The Tavistock Institute

In experimental group work at Leicester University, I convinced my team to withhold information that would effectively allow us to take control of the proceedings. A tad subversive perhaps, but it worked and technically we *won* the exercise. In this training forum, there was absolutely nothing material at stake. But the pushback from the other groups against our 'crime' was monumental. We had broken the group norms and the negative feedback was loud, vociferous and almost personally threatening. And this in a forum where we were supposed to experiment with process and 'leadership' (many people work to a definition of leadership that is fiercely conservative).

Family Patterns

In work organisations, we learn to conform, to go along, to 'not speak up'. Otherwise, we risk being ostracised. Exactly as most of us learned to behave in our first organisation: the family. Most of us are programmed to conform from an early age – and learn that lesson all too well. This is reinforced when we go to work and are re-programmed to be conservative for a second time. This idea has a particular relevance to the current debate on the reform of the public sector.

Public Sector

Historically, senior public servants played a game that could be labelled as 'Mind the Minister'. If they had an opposing view to the Minister's view, it was seldom committed to paper. I am convinced that some future academic study will reveal that the enactment of the *Freedom of Information Act* will have succeeded in burying more information than it has released – as it has pushed 'alternative viewpoints' 30,000 feet underground. Nothing is now committed to paper.

Second, the seniority system is based on time served – rather than breakthrough thinking. In the UK, they refer to this system of promotion as 'Buggin's turn'. In order to get promoted, you learn to keep your head below the parapet – very much in keeping with the Japanese maxim:

The nail that sticks up gets hammered down.

The combined effects of a family culture in which we 'learn our place' and a workplace culture where we 'keep our place' have conspired to disallow challenges to the *status quo*. We make changes 'at the margins' and only then by consensus. Our goal is to achieve 'buy in', elevating the *process* of leadership to a higher platform than the *result* – hence the 'process morons' comment by Wren referred to earlier.

Inner Leader

The challenge for each of us is clear. Practice being an adult at work – rather than an overgrown schoolchild following orders. Start with a personal revolution against stupid work practices that no longer make sense (I'm working on the assumption here that you actually want to make a difference). Do it, even if it's just to escape the boredom. Release your inner leader! **Don't be a smart person, continuing to do stupid things**. And sometimes I even take my own advice!

DON'T BE A DUMMY TWICE: IF YOU MAKE A MISTAKE, ADMIT IT

Sometimes, you get a rush of blood to the head and want to try something completely different. Trying new stuff on holidays works well for me. Last year, it was the short-lived experiment of growing a beard (I ended up looking like Jedward's Granddad). This year, it was renting a motorbike.

Winnipeg Experience

The last time I had access to a big motorbike was in Canada exactly 38 years ago. I was 18, and I drove around for a month without incident. I had another motorbike in Ireland for a couple of years after that, before graduating to a car. But surely I would remember how to control it. It's like riding a bike, right? And I was only ever involved in three accidents… The logic was impeccable. You have to keep pushing the edge of the envelope. Otherwise, you might be getting 'set in your ways'!

Instant Reaction

My buddy Maurice offered a mild opinion on this adventure, framed as follows:

> You f*****g gobshite.

He thought it was completely nuts because of:

- Portuguese roads.
- Portuguese drivers.
- The length of time since I was within 100 yards of a motorbike.

I took all the feedback on board, thought about it seriously for all of 12.2 seconds, then went on the Internet and booked a Honda Rebel 250cc bike for a week. What could possibly go wrong?

Cometh the Hour

It was late July, 34 degrees centigrade. I was dressed in a tracksuit and melting with the heat, standing nervously outside the bike rental shop in Albuifeira, about 15 miles from where we were staying. The mission was as follows: pick up the bike and drive along the EN-125 (the busiest road in the Algarve) to 'prove' that I was not over the hill. A combination of perspiration and suntan oil was running down my face, stinging my eyes. But, I couldn't possibly quit now. Not after telling Linda and the kids. Cool dad, eh? And, most importantly, to prove Maurice wrong. There was no way I was wimping out.

So, I figured out how the gears worked (one down, five up) and drove out along the main road. Slowly. The traffic jam behind me stretched back up to near Lisbon! By the time I eventually got to where we were staying, I'd made an executive decision: turn around and take it back. Admit defeat. I'm past the motorbike stage in my life.

The Moral

Sometimes, you make a wrong call. For a variety of good or bad reasons. But you know yourself that's it's a bad call. A job that hasn't worked out. A relationship that's soured. A house that really does not suit your family. Whatever. What you need to do is fix it.

Even if it means that you look stupid. You know it's right. Now, not all mistakes are as easy to fix as bringing back that motorbike. But **all mistakes have to be confronted. Don't let your ego stop you from making the right call**.

Postscript: Maurice's' response:

I told you that you were too old for that.

Ouch!

DON'T BE AN OSTRICH: ASK "HOW AM I REALLY DOING?"

Sometimes managers, despite their best efforts, seem to be blocked from making progress. They work long hours and deliver projects on time / budget. But somehow the 'golden ticket to the executive club' is not forthcoming. And the reason is... *they... don't know what the reason is.*

In coaching sessions, mid-level managers show me copies of *solid* performance appraisals. They relate positive 'pat on the back' conversations with the CEO or board members - but somehow, they never seem to make the cut. The glass ceiling (which applies to both men and women) acts as an invisible barrier to progress. The key question: Is there some way to find out what's really holding you back? Would it be possible to find a pair of 'X-ray spectacles' to help you see what's happening? Well, it turns out that this is available...

Self-deception

Many of us, whether we admit it or not, see ourselves in a slightly more positive light than others see us. Assuming that the people we work with are objective, they see our good points but they also detect flaws in the diamond. Asking the question "How am I really doing?" - to bosses, peers and subordinates - is an antidote to the problem of self-deception. Understanding exactly how you are seen in the organisation is, arguably, the key to career success.

There are a number of reasons why it's a good idea to ask, "How am I really doing?" – a very different question from "How am I doing?", often a thinly-disguised code for "Tell me all the things that you like about me and where I'm doing great".

Staff Love It

They may be a little shocked when you ask, even suspicious. One manager related an interesting story. After he asked the question, an employee looked sceptically at him, then looked all around the room, and finally said, "Are we on *Candid Camera*?"

Whatever the initial reaction, employees love it when they're asked to support their boss with this question (assuming that they believe the question is sincere).

Gets Information

Managers are typically insulated from real feedback – people don't tell them how they are doing. Even where formal systems of performance management are in place, they fear that this will potentially open up a minefield. So, a lot of senior managers steer a middle course and avoid anything that is 'sensitive'. In online 360-degree surveys, respondents score everything as '3' (out of 5), taking the middle ground. They avoid *pointed* (potentially useful) feedback that might identify them.

Just asking the question doesn't necessarily mean your boss will open up and provide candid feedback. But if you set the tone right and do a good job of listening to the responses, you'll hear things you've never heard before – about how you are seen and what you could do to become more productive. When you ask a number of people who know you well, common themes start to emerge. You can almost feel that glass starting to splinter.

Sometimes Painful

Sometimes an employee's poor work performance is related to *your* performance as a manager. For example, if you are losing employees' respect because you won't confront an obvious problem that's making *their* lives miserable, it'll affect motivation. Or, perhaps employees resent you because you're always pointing out mistakes (without balancing this by telling them what they're doing right). The trick is to find out what you're doing that's 'irritating' staff, and then correct it.

Assuming you've the guts to do this, it can be a hugely beneficial exercise. It's not for everyone and not for all situations. But it can work, really well in some cases. Some managers stick their head in the sand. They believe that all problems are temporary and will go away if ignored for long enough. Or they 'outsource' the blame - "If only I had a better PA, finance manager (or whatever)".

Don't be an ostrich. **While the process of discovering a bit more about yourself can be painful, it's normally a *growing* pain, a path that leads to a better version of yourself**. Isn't that what we are all chasing?

GET SOME 'R&R': BUILDING ROUTINES AND RESILIENCE

The Hunt for My Pullover

In Ireland, we call them 'pullovers' or 'jumpers'. Preferably made from pure wool, it's the single best way to keep the damp at bay, during the nine-month weather period (October to June) in Ireland when the major meteorological change is the intensity of the rain.

Purple Rain

On this particular Tuesday, I definitely needed a pullover. It had been raining steadily for 22 hours. The wind was howling in from somewhere east of St. Petersburg. To make matters worse, I'd forgotten to put the office heat on 'timer' and the place was colder than a polar bear's testicle. Chained to the computer to finish a report, I was feeling sorry for myself. Whatever the opposite of a 'purple patch' is, this was it. Something had to be done. Fast.

No Chocolate

It was mid-way through the Catholic period known as Lent – the six-week run-in to Easter. While no-one in our house is religious, Linda keeps a fasting *tradition* going as a form of self-discipline – with a complete ban on chocolate during Lent.

It's a hard rule to enforce. For example, I could just top up the petrol in the car every day and have a sneaky Mars bar in the garage seven times a week during refills. But, that solution seems like hard work.

Meanwhile, Linda keeps herself busy – buying multiple Easter eggs for our kids / her nieces / nephews / mother and stacking them in full view on the mantelpiece in the 'good room'. And, like that Oscar Wilde quip:

> *I can resist anything except temptation.*

On such a gloomy day, I definitely needed a fix.

The Raid

The most important thing when launching a stealth mission is to bear in mind the 11th Commandment: *Thou shall not get caught.* While this may sound self-congratulatory, it actually required quite a bit of dexterity: manoeuvring my left hand through the tiny gap in the bottom of a Galaxy Easter egg and wriggling out the enclosed packet of Minstrels. A slight bend, but not a single tear in the cardboard box. Result!

However, the main problem with chocolate is that it tastes like *more*. Outside, the rain was lashing down, with not a glimmer of hope. There was nothing else for it – but to go back in again. You have to be brave. That's what I always say!

Reflection Time

Answer me this: Have you ever (since you were 7+ years old) eaten a huge Easter egg in a single sitting, wolfing it down in case anyone entered the room and you'd be caught red-handed? I felt queasy for about 12 hours afterwards – the potent combination of an upset stomach intertwined with remorse about being weak-willed.

Hey, I'm guessing that your empathy may not be in overdrive right now. Perhaps you are busily recalling the wonderfully evocative phrase:

Serves you f***ing right!

Managerial Discipline

Great managers, in my experience, are highly disciplined. Of course, there's some genius about – people able to foretell market futures, invent computing languages or come up with something equally exotic. But most managerial careers are built on discipline, not inspiration. Woody Allen said:

80% percent of success is just showing up.

I believe it. **You start by learning to manage yourself and you eventually lead others**. So, how exactly do you 'manage yourself'?

Routines and Resilience

By developing routine processes and sticking to them. By working hard and 'trusting that the process will deliver'. By taking account of what other people say and coming back to them – whether the answer is a "Yes" or a "No". By positive self-talk that doesn't allow you to be moany, embracing a 'woe-is-me' narrative, becoming addicted to your own misery. And by resisting metaphorical Easter eggs that come in the shape of 'sick days', taking it 'handy' or otherwise slacking off the rope. William Wallace said: "Every man dies, but not every man truly lives". (I'll make the working assumption that he meant that to apply to women too.)

Most of the successful people I've bumped up against to date have two things in common. The first is that they exercise personal discipline. Hard work. Routine. Focus. The second thing is that they don't buckle when (some) things inevitably go south. They have mastered the art of resilience – by building on previous triumphs (which are like credits in the bank) and by understanding that not everything in life goes swimmingly well. They know that 92% is as good as it gets.

Cast Iron?

It's not a cast-iron success formula. Some people deal with awful health issues, for themselves or close family members. Accidents can ruin lives. And so on. The notion that we have full control is a myth. But the opposite notion – that we have *no* control – is a much more destructive myth. **If you can develop a powerful routine and wrap some personal resilience around it, you are well on the road to success**. The bonus is that you'll be as happy as a hammer in a nail factory.

Too Late?

Perhaps it seems too late to start all this stuff? You might be 30, or 40, or 53 and feel that things haven't gone so well to date? May I suggest that you steal shamelessly JK Rowling's line:

> *Rock bottom became the solid foundation on which I rebuilt my life.*

So, how should you respond when someone says they don't believe this 'You are the CEO of your own life' bullshit? Tell them (honestly) that you've yet to meet a rich cynic!

BECOME A BRILLIANT DELEGATOR

A slightly longer piece this time on an important topic that has a huge impact on personal productivity. If you could 'fix' one thing this year, this just might be it. *Core Idea:* There's no such thing as a single-handed success. We all need help now and again. If you're really serious about becoming a powerful player, you need to learn to delegate. Now, buckle in for the science!

Richard Branson

Here's how Richard Branson once described the importance of delegation:

> *Imagine you're a professional juggler. As a novice, you start juggling and slowly increase the number of balls to help draw a larger crowd. As the crowd increases, so do their expectations. You start adding more difficult items like pins. It's going well. Sometimes you drop a ball but you continue and your audience slowly grows. Then you decide to move to riskier stuff, adding flaming arrows and chainsaws. The crowd loves what you do and you want to keep all the elements going (balls, pins, flaming arrows and chainsaws). But the risk is getting very high now. If you drop a ball, it's fine. But drop a chainsaw and you'll*

end up in a wheelchair. So, what do you do? You delegate. You hire an assistant to take the easy stuff out of your hands (balls and pins) and leave you with the important stuff (flaming arrows and chainsaws). If they drop a ball now and then, it's not that big a deal. Just teach them what they need to change. Before you know it, you'll no longer have to worry about them dropping anything.

Perhaps you don't buy the juggling analogy? Here's some more arguments in favour of building your skills in this area.

Time-poor

Time is the most precious commodity for executives. No matter how hard you work, you can't do everything by yourself. Leveraging time has always been the 'X Factor' in executive success. If you're feeling overworked, stressed, or falling behind, chances are that you are holding onto more responsibilities or tasks than is reasonable. *Key question:* **Who else could do this?**

Full Headlights

As you move up the organisation, senior executives watch to see not just whether you get the job done, but also *how* you get it done. They want leadership skills demonstrated with a focus on the future. Mid-ranking executives often spend too much time dealing with immediate problems, and not enough time working strategically on process improvements and building organisational capability. Delegation allows you the space to work 'on' the business (rather than being continually sucked 'into' it). *Key question:* **Can you switch from dipped onto full headlights and look further out the road?**

Developing Managers

Your job = getting the 'next generation' of managers ready for a bigger role. Adults learn by doing – not by hearing or seeing – but by getting involved in the action. Remember that old line:

You go to college to do your MBA, then go to work to learn the rest of the alphabet.

Delegation allows senior people to leverage their time and offers developmental opportunities to junior managers. *Key question:* **Are you investing any real effort in this?**

Great Idea

But here's a killer question: if delegation is such a great idea, how come it's not used much? There are several reasons to explain why executives avoid delegation. Do any of these apply to you?

- ◆ Some executives have never seen delegation in action and don't really understand how it works.
- ◆ Others have a negative experience of senior managers pushing the 'crap' parts of their job downwards, labelling laziness as delegation.
- ◆ Those of a perfectionist bent often hold the view that 'if you want something done right, do it yourself'. They never learn to let go and some actually compete with their managers to show them 'how it should be done' (the managerial equivalent of 'mine is bigger than yours'). The result = junior managers become more and more dependent, and less able to act on their own.
- ◆ Perhaps you enjoy doing particular tasks and don't want to give them away; you just wish you had more time to do them all. Executives who don't get satisfaction from watching their managers succeed might actually be

happier in individual contributor roles. *Career advice:* Go back to being an engineer or an accountant – don't clog up that senior role where the expectation is that you will manage differently than you did 10 or 15 years ago.

♦ Sometimes executives feel that managers are already under pressure and are reluctant to assign more work, for fear of overloading them. If your managers think that you are dumping on them, this might well be the case. But where you communicate that delegation is part of your philosophy to help them grow, this is pretty unlikely.

♦ Finally, there are a small number of executives who fear delegating on the basis of being outshone by their staff. There probably is no cure for this group; they should be rounded up at the back of the factory and shot!

Three Steps to Success

To delegate effectively, you need to do three things:

♦ Choose the *right tasks* to delegate.

♦ Identify the *right people* to delegate to.

♦ Delegate in the *right way*.

Complex? Not really, albeit it does take practice. Just remember that the potential prize is huge. Here's how to make it work.

Step #1: Choose the Right Tasks to Delegate

Check your diary (or ask your PA to do this) over the past month or so. Review what you are actually doing and how long you spend at individual tasks. When a task is scattered throughout the day or week or month, executives often seriously underestimate how much time they spend at it. Remember, when you're doing, you're not managing. Instead, you're attending to tasks that could be handled by lower-cost people. The principle is division of labour – **work should be done by people best qualified to do it at the least expense to the organisation**.

And there's a second subtle point at play here. As an executive, you are not just another manager. You are a coach. Coaches understand the importance of teaching, motivating, and taking pride in the performance of others. It's **moving away from** *managing* **(focusing on what needs to be done today) towards** *leading* **(what you are trying to build tomorrow)**. Get those headlights onto a blue beam!

Ask yourself: "How much of the work that I currently do myself would I hand off to my managers if I were comfortable that this would be completed within quality parameters?" When asked this question, many executives respond that they would hand off up to 50% of their workload.

Here's how to choose the right tasks to delegate:

- ♦ **Eliminate it:** All too often, work continues to be done because it has always been done. If you set aside time to review your work, you will probably find opportunities to streamline processes and procedures. Don't delegate anything that can be eliminated.
- ♦ **Repeat tasks:** Delegate tasks you do over and over. You've probably mastered them, but managers could learn new skills by completing these tasks.
- ♦ **Complete jobs:** Try to delegate complete jobs, rather than portions. It gives managers the chance to come up with creative solutions from start to finish and feel a sense of ownership and pride about their work.
- ♦ **Long deadlines:** Delegate tasks that don't have immediate deadlines. These provide good opportunities for managers to learn without too much time pressure.

- **Mission-critical:** Would a failure de-rail the business? If it's a 'bet the farm' project, don't hand it over to someone else.

Of course, not everything can be delegated. Sometimes you're in charge of a project because of your particular expertise and DIY is the best bet. If a project is confidential, it may not be possible to outsource it. And some jobs, by their very nature, need to be done by the person sitting in the executive seat ("Excuse me, Theresa. After lunch, could you inform George that he's fired? Thanks, I really appreciate it").

So, let's assume that you have segmented your job into two columns: the bits that you can do and those elements that you can safely ask someone else to tackle. What happens next?

Step #2: Choose the Right People to Delegate to

Not all managers are created equally. Before you hive off a chunk of work, consider your managers' skill level, motivation and dependability. Matching the person and the task is more art than science; start small and be patient. **When you find the right person for the work in question, everybody wins**.

Here's how to choose the right person for the task:

- **Showing potential:** Have particular people shown an appetite to move up a level? Encourage them by giving them 'chunks' of your current job to complete.
- **Skilling up:** Delegate a task to a manager who needs to work on particular skills (awkwardness at running meetings, failure to meet deadlines, etc). Use delegation to help the manager overcome the obstacle and advance their career.

Step #3: Delegate in the Right Way

How many times have you been given a job where the first thing you need to figure out is "What exactly am I supposed to do here?". **When you are assigning unfamiliar tasks, be specific in explaining what you need, the expected quality standard and timelines**. Detailing an assignment (in writing) leaves less room for error based on misunderstanding.

It's really useful to use a standard format, which should include:

- Description (what you want done).
- Purpose (how it fits into the overall business goals.
- Timelines (milestones for checking in).
- Authority (the type of decisions that can be made).
- Resources.

A standard format will help you to become adept at quickly delegating tasks to others and will become part of your managerial toolkit. It's much easier than 're-inventing' the 'form' each time you want to delegate a project.

When you delegate a task, remember that you retain accountability for the successful completion of the work. **To delegate is to trade one kind of work for another: you still have to manage, coach, and appraise**.

The key steps are:

- **End results:** Remember that you are delegating responsibilities, not methods. It's OK to talk about techniques you've found helpful, but not every person will do the job the same way (the manager may find a better way to do the job). Focus on results.
- **Project control:** Explain how performance will be measured and the level of accountability that comes with

the task. We know we shouldn't micro-manage. However, this doesn't mean we abdicate control. In effective delegation, we have to find the (sometimes difficult) balance between providing space for people to use their own abilities, while monitoring to ensure that the job is done correctly.

- **Bite-sized:** Large projects may be easier to monitor if they are broken into smaller segments where staff report to you after each segment is completed. Doing this daily, weekly, or monthly will help you keep on track. If the Dublin to Cork train does not reach Portlaoise in an hour, Irish Rail knows that something has gone amiss. A similar review mechanism will keep your projects on track. Staying informed limits the possibility of failure.

- **Staff coaching:** When you delegate an assignment, make it clear that managers can come to you with questions. New tasks are always confusing. Be patient and 'catch people doing something right' to build their confidence. Research clearly demonstrates that people live up (or down) to our expectations. It's important to realise how your support and expressed confidence can help a manager succeed. Equally, hesitation, even if never stated verbally, can undermine a positive outcome.

- **Be patient:** When you first start to delegate, the manager will take longer than you do to complete tasks. You are an expert in the field and the person you have delegated to is still learning. If you've chosen the right person and you are delegating correctly, he or she will quickly become competent. Be patient.

- **Full acceptance:** When delegated work is delivered to you, set aside enough time to review it thoroughly. Only accept high quality, fully-completed work. If you accept work where you're not satisfied, the manager does not learn to do the job properly. Worse, you accept a new tranche of work that you will need to complete yourself. Of course, when good work is returned, make sure you recognise and reward the effort. Give managers the recognition they deserve and don't (this is a huge No No) take credit for their work.

- **Post-mortems:** Ask the manager to reflect on 'lessons learned'. It's important for them to know that you will tolerate imperfection. Encourage them to be open and learn from their mistakes. Ask: "What are the two most important insights you've gained from this experience?" and "What would you do differently next time out?"

Is It Worth It?

At first glance, delegation might feel like more hassle than it's worth. And that would be… a major mistake. Some years back, I saw a cartoon that depicted a medieval battle scene where the soldiers were fighting using longbows and swords. Just off the battlefield, one of the soldiers was explaining a new technology (a machine-gun) to the king who said:

> *I don't have time for this newfangled stuff, we have a battle to fight.*

If you want to put rocket fuel on your own career, learn how to delegate effectively. **Become a productivity legend while getting most of your work done by others**. Now, what's not to like about that idea?

Section 3:
BRILLIANT
COMMUNICATIONS

ARE YOU A GREAT FACILIATOR?

Every now and then a breakthrough idea occurs to me, something that really changes my consulting life. The BIG idea today is that... great facilitators have groundrules and skip lunch.

Who Owns the Monkey?

Facilitators are normally asked to work with individuals or groups who are struggling to resolve current issues (remedial agenda) or looking further out the road to unravel some future mystery (developmental agenda). In both cases, there is a 'task' to be completed. It's my job to help the client achieve their goal and, hopefully, to have a bit of fun along the way. Business does not have to be boring.

Unsettling Tasks

Now, depending on the task and the people in the room, topics can be quite confusing, even *unsettling*. For example, the other day I was talking with a very successful guy who owns a large car dealership. He wanted to (big surprise here) sell more cars. But the fact that the Irish economy tanked had dinted his plans and there was no sign of relief on the horizon. As the size of the 'cake' is relatively fixed due to macro-economic factors (outside of his control), I moved the topic onto how he might increase the *portion* of cake that his business gets. Among a range of topics, we discussed the role of social media in marketing, how 'conversations' with his current clients and potential clients might help him sell more cars in the future. Turns out that this guy, a mechanic by training, does not use a computer and is quite a technophobe. So, he found this part of the conversation 'uneasy' and did not want to discuss it at all. The 'minutes' of our conversation would read as follows:

> *Let's just go back to the Celtic Tiger when I sold shedloads of cars without having to learn any new stuff.*

Underpinning Anxiety

At meetings to discuss today's presenting issues or future problems, the debates are seldom linear and there can be all sorts of discomfort. When individuals or groups experience ideas that 'challenge' their current thinking (what psychologists call *dissonance*), their instinct is to 'close the conversation down'. To ease the anxiety, they want to stop the debate or make a quick decision, anything that helps to move away from the *discomfort* of the topic. But, because learning often comes 'close to the edge of the cliff', my role as a facilitator is to help the group to *stay with the discomfort* for as long as possible. How? I've found two techniques really work well:

- ◆ Having groundrules.
- ◆ Skipping lunch.

Having Groundrules

The idea of having some 'groundrules' for a meeting is hardly revolutionary – but it's surprising how many meetings kick off without these being agreed in advance. There is no 'single set' of groundrules that works for every meeting – they need to be customised to the topic – but here's a couple of ideas that I've found useful:

- Being co-operative and non-competitive (company hat, not functional hat).
- Creating a safe, supportive and trusting climate (OK to say: "I don't know").
- Being non-defensive about your area or your people.
- Being vulnerable (open to areas of chaos, confusion and lack of skill).
- Participation in the workshop (under- and over-participation are both venial sins).
- Adopting a spirit of enquiry without dogmatism and authoritarianism.
- Enjoying ourselves (no ban on humour – as long as it's not an escape hatch).
- Confidentiality (affirming, "We are in Lodge").

You don't have to arrive with a pre-cooked list; ask the participants to help you develop this at the front end of the meeting (if time allows).

Skipping Lunch

The second rule when acting as a facilitator is that I normally skip lunch (and not JUST because of weight issues). I usually work through lunch to pull together the strands of the morning session, which I then present to the group when they come back. This allows the group to get a sense of the progress made. Sometimes, when it seems that we were 'rambling all over the place', pulling the various strands together helps make sense of the discussion and provides a sense of forward movement. I always feel that they are paying for facilitation (task accomplishment) not empathy. **The market for "I feel your pain" is limited in commercial organisations; results pay the bills**.

A couple of weeks back, at the end of a particularly difficult two-day session, one of the participants said to me:

> *You have such a handy job. All you do is show up and listen, get people to talk to each other and then summarise what they've said.*

I smiled. Like good golf, when my job looks really easy, I know that I'm playing well.

Today's Question

Are you a great facilitator? There is probably a brilliant facilitator in there, just waiting to get out. Release the beast. It's amazing what you can achieve when you don't need to get credit for it.

GREAT LEADERS ARE
GREAT TEACHERS

I'm in the thick of training our new puppy, Louie. At almost three months old, he looks cute and is really smart. He will eventually turn into a big dog, so a few fundamentals need to be welded into place. First, a dog has to learn to walk on the lead without dragging you along; the owner walks the dog, not *vice versa* (assuming that you don't want to end up with arms like Magilla Gorilla). Second, the dog has to understand basic commands (Sit, Stay and Down) so that you can maintain control when he's off the lead. There is more advanced obedience stuff and all sorts of agility work – but that's typically beyond what the 'normal' dog owner wants.

Who's Your Daddy?

Because dogs are pack animals, they look for a *leader* and you need to assert yourself into this role. One lady I know got a puppy, on loan, from the Guide Dogs for the Blind. She wanted to test-drive owning a dog to see how the kids reacted. They couldn't manage him. She described the return trip to the Marine Hotel in Sutton, with the dog sitting on her lap trying to eat the steering wheel as she drove along the Coast Road! So, a dog has to know that you are the boss. It's the doggie equivalent of Steve Staunton famously telling the Irish soccer team, "I'm the gaffer". (Note to Steve: If you have to tell them, you're not!)

Training Rules

In simple terms, the three rules of dog instruction are:

- ♦ Digestible chunks.
- ♦ Positive reinforcement.
- ♦ Endless patience.

Now, if you don't find the metaphor too offensive, it turns out that those rules work quite well for training people too. But, much more importantly than any particular 'technique' is the core idea that **teaching is a central leadership activity**.

Why? Because it contains two divine ideas in a single behaviour. It helps to 're-skill' the next generation of managers (*Newsflash:* you may be training the CEO of NAMA *circa* 2020). Second, it signals a real commitment to helping people to grow professionally. Not just talking about this, but putting your diary (time) where your mouth is.

Success Secrets

Over the past 20 years or so, I've asked countless executives about the 'secret' of their success. It's amazing how many highlight the importance of a particular teacher or mentor in their rise to glory and how much they appreciated this (then and now). Yet some senior executives think that teaching is 'below their pay grade' – to be delegated to the HR function or outsourced. At best, they might cover the cost of this (the 'cheque-book' school of management). But they would never *dirty their own hands* with this low-level activity. That's a mistake.

Blackjack and Craps

Great teaching is a thing of beauty. And it doesn't have to be boring. On the face of it, teaching your kids to gamble might not seem like a great idea. But if you want your kids to study maths and work hard at it, then this is a brilliant way to introduce probability theory. Kids (and adults) want to learn useful skills and are engaged when they can see how to apply them. I spend all my working life coaching and problem-solving organisation issues with executives. It's a hugely positive activity (I haven't got the skills to work effectively with kids; remember the old joke: "I wanted to be a doctor, but I didn't have the patience").

Sustainable Leadership

My overall sense is that leadership, like green energy, should be a sustainable concept. It's not just what you achieve while you are 'in the chair', but what you leave in place when you've departed. And training the next generation of managers / leaders is a powerful legacy, even if it seems a bit 'wussy' to those who believe that powerful leaders come straight from central casting in

Hollywood – the "Follow me, I always know what I am doing" types.

Leading by Teaching

In your effort to become the world's foremost executive (that's a good thing), you need to maintain your humanity. The Queen supposedly thought that every factory smelled of paint (not realising that every factory had been painted just before her arrival). In similar vein, many leaders get disconnected from reality. Getting down and dirty with your team (by teaching them), or muddling through stuff together (showing your own vulnerability), is one of the hallmarks of a leader with great connect skills.

In the meantime, if you see someone in Clontarf with a pocket bulging with dog biscuits shouting "Good boy, Come" in a falsetto voice, don't be alarmed. It's only me teaching Louie new tricks. And from time to time, we all need a few of those!

ACTIVE LISTENING: THE ULTIMATE COMMUNICATIONS SKILL?

Over the years, I have been involved in teaching communications skills to hundreds of executives. The most common issue is where senior managers are uncomfortable or unconvincing when speaking in public. For a small number of executives, this is phobia territory. The comedian Jerry Seinfeld remarked:

At a funeral, most people would prefer to be in the box than to give the eulogy.

Presentation Skills

The good news is that presentation skills can be learned. Like touch-typing or windsurfing, it takes a bit of practice, but once you understand the basic rules, you get the hang of it. While not everyone will morph into a great public speaker (some of it is driven by personality type), almost everyone can become a solid performer. Let's tick that box and move on.

To Write or Not to Write

The second communication skill is writing. Many executives dislike writing; some actively avoid it. They might be OK on emails and shorter stuff – but have a real distaste for writing reports or constructing strategy documents where arguments have to be marshalled in a particular way. In terms of curability, writing skills can also be honed. While we may not be able to convert CEOs emails into thrillers, it's usually possible to spot the bigger writing mistakes and eradicate these. For sure, some practice is needed, but good writing is also a learned craft.

Interestingly, the 'market' for helping executives improve their writing skills is quite small. It's as if acknowledging a writing deficit is somehow a greater sin than being a poor presenter. So, even executives who know they don't write well (and not everyone is self-aware) find it hard to ask for help with this. Can you see that we're on a roll here? The good news with both presentation and writing skills is that they can be fixed - provided that the will exists to put in the sweat equity. And this leads us neatly to the single BIGGEST executive skills deficit: poor listening.

Active Listening

I've written elsewhere (*Accidental Leadership*, The Liffey Press, 2009) that **there is an inverse relationship between organisation level and listening skills**. The general rule is as follows: as you become more senior, you listen less. You hog the conversation. You interrupt when others are speaking. People listen to you, not because what you say is insightful or funny; they listen to you because of your stripes. It's a tribal thing. You are more senior in the tribe (an 'elder') and are given the respect for this.

Poor Listening De-rails Careers

I worked with a well-respected executive who held the CEO role in an Irish subsidiary. He'd sought coaching on 'cultural sensitivity' – because he did not seem to be able to curry influence within the USA parent company. Very effective in Ireland, he felt that he was 'missing' some key information when he travelled to the US and met with his counterparts. After meeting him a couple of times, the 'problem' was re-diagnosed as follows. He was a terrible listener. This did not hold him back in Ireland – because his subordinates tolerated this. He'd simply have to lean forward in a meeting or lose eye contact and people would respond – watching and interpreting his body language. Yet, his poor listening skills almost upended his career when he had to interact with his peer CEOs (country managers) when they all met at HQ. This group were much less tolerant of his 'interruptions' and failure to understand their perspective of the world. It was not a cultural sensitivity issue – it was a bad case of poor listening.

Listening is Not Waiting

Some senior executives don't listen at all. They simply wait – until the other person finishes what they are saying – and then they continue to speak. People sometimes have two separate conversations – what the Jesuit writer, John Powell, labelled as a 'dialogue of the deaf'. The key downside is that when you are talking, you are not understanding and seldom learning. Poor listening cuts off a huge amount of data within your organisation, about the external competition, etc.

Of course, there are times to be forceful, to ague vehemently, to confidently defend a position. But, there are a far greater number of times to listen, to show empathy, to discover, to allow contradictory ideas make you uncomfortable. We all know the line:

God gave you two ears and one mouth so you should listen twice as much as you speak.

Do you?

In Denial

For many executives, admitting to being a poor listener is akin to saying that you are tight with money, are a poor judge of character or are completely useless in the sack. In my experience, executives tend to overestimate their ability in this area. And, if you are an extrovert, your listening skills are usually worse again. Your default style is to be centre stage, as extroverts use talking as a way of thinking *("How do I know what I believe? I haven't said it yet")*. I should know. I have to continually fight a poor listening style and keep this under control (sometimes, it even works!).

Protecting Yourself

Poor listening can be a form of self-protection. We are bombarded with information that challenges our worldview. Customer defections, declining markets, game-changing technology and smart competitor moves assault our security. When we hear that an idea or project we are personally invested in has gone south, our instinct is to blank it out. We hear the noise, but 'filter' the bad news.

But, the really good news is that poor listening can be fixed. There are a myriad of training techniques (many developed in the area of counselling and psychotherapy) that can lift your listening game. Active listening is actually a number of distinct 'mini-skills', which you can learn, practice and get better at.

How good are you in the listening space and how much do you want to improve this? Listening is the ultimate communications skill for executives and is vastly undervalued.

Are you listening?

IS THIS THE BEST SPEECH EVER MADE?

Happy Days

Without a shadow of doubt, the happiest event in the university calendar is graduation day. The students line up with their parents and families to celebrate past achievements and look forward to the future. Sometimes, they ask a guest speaker to participate. The following is from Pulitzer Prize-winning author Anna Quindlen's commencement address to Villanova University. Normally I don't simply repeat what other people have said. But, sometimes, the original is so good that it needs no embellishment. Happy to let Anna do all the heavy lifting this time. Here's what she said:

> *It's a great honor for me to be the third member of my family to receive an honorary doctorate from this great university. It's an honor to follow my great-uncle Jim, who was a gifted physician, and my Uncle Jack, who is a remarkable businessman. Both of them could have told you something important about their professions, about medicine or commerce. I have no specialized field of interest or expertise, which puts me at a disadvantage, talking to you today.*
>
> *I'm a novelist. My work is human nature. Real life is all I know. Don't ever confuse the two, your life and your*

*work. You will walk out of here this afternoon with only
one thing that no-one else has. There will be
hundreds of people out there with your same degree:
there will be thousands of people doing what you
want to do for a living. But you will be the only person
alive who has sole custody of your life. Your particular
life. Your entire life. Not just your life at a desk or your
life on a bus or in a car or at the computer. Not just the
life of your mind, but the life of your heart. Not just
your bank accounts but also your soul. People don't
talk about the soul very much anymore. It's so much
easier to write a resume than to craft a spirit. But a
resume is cold comfort on a winter's night, or when
you're sad, or broke, or lonely, or when you've
received your test results and they're not so good.*

*Here is my resume: I am a good mother to three
children. I have tried never to let my work stand in the
way of being a good parent. I no longer consider
myself the centre of the universe. I show up. I listen. I
try to laugh. I am a good friend to my husband. I have
tried to make marriage vows mean what they say. I am
a good friend to my friends and them to me. Without
them, there would be nothing to say to you today,
because I would be a cardboard cut-out. But I call
them on the phone and I meet them for lunch. I would
be rotten, at best mediocre, at my job if those other
things were not true.*

*You cannot be really first rate at your work if your work
is all you are. So, here's what I wanted to tell you
today: Get a life. A real life, not a manic pursuit of the*

next promotion, the bigger pay cheque, the larger house. Do you think you'd care so very much about those things if you blew an aneurysm one afternoon or found a lump in your breast?

Get a life in which you notice the smell of salt water pushing itself on a breeze at the seaside, a life in which you stop and watch how a red-tailed hawk circles over the water, or the way a baby scowls with concentration when she tries to pick up a sweet with her thumb and first finger.

Get a life in which you are not alone. Find people you love, and who love you. And remember that love is not leisure, it is work. Pick up the phone. Send an email. Write a letter. Get a life in which you are generous. And realize that life is the best thing ever, and that you have no business taking it for granted. Care so deeply about its goodness that you want to spread it around. Take money you would have spent on beer and give it to charity. Work in a soup kitchen. Be a big brother or sister. All of you want to do well. But if you do not do good too, then doing well will never be enough.

It is so easy to waste our lives, our days, our hours, and our minutes. It is so easy to take for granted the color of our kids' eyes, the way the melody in a symphony rises and falls and disappears and rises again. It is so easy to exist instead of to live.

I learned to live many years ago. I learned to love the journey, not the destination. I learned that it is not a dress rehearsal, and that today is the only guarantee you get. I learned to look at all the good in the world and try to give some of it back because I believed in it, completely and utterly. And I tried to do that, in part, by telling others what I had learned. By telling them this: Consider the lilies of the field. Look at the fuzz on a baby's ear. Read in the back yard with the sun on your face.

Learn to be happy. And think of life as a terminal illness, because if you do, you will live it with joy and passion as it ought to be lived.

Wow!

Mindfulness (living in the present moment) is probably the hottest topic in counselling right now. Anna's speech addresses mindfulness in a very powerful and evocative way. Lessons here for all of us.

Seize the day!

WANT TO BE SUCCESSFUL? LEARN HOW TO MAKE GREAT PRESENTATIONS

In this business, we get involved in all sorts of events. Have laptop, will travel. So, the call to make a presentation on coaching to the Irish Midwives conference in Galway wasn't particularly unusual. On the basis that you can never become complacent, I needed something to grab audience attention right up front. While the first 100 days sets the tone for a political career, the first 100 seconds are critically important in effective presentations. When he did shows with American soldiers stationed overseas, Bob Hope always completed preliminary reconnaissance. He'd find out something quirky about the commanding officer. Then he'd build that into an opening joke and have the audience eating out of his hand. While not many people have Bob Hope's *delivery*, we can all steal shamelessly from the method.

Phone a Friend

In times of crisis, you turn to your friends, right? As it happens, one of my music buddies, Sean Dowling, is a midwife in the Rotunda (apparently, there are three male midwives working there. Who would have known?). I explained the dilemma and he promised to come back with the answer. During the follow-up conversation, Sean was excited. "I have it, I have it", he declared. "You walk on stage to the James Bond soundtrack and declare:

'Paul Mooney, at your cervix.'" With friends like Sean, who needs enemies?

Googling like crazy, I came up with the line "I'm a midwife. What's your superpower?" and ran with that instead (#chicken).

Humour Works

Humour works well – up to a point. Right up to the edge of the cliff, it works really great. Go just beyond that and the fall is steep.

One time, I sat in the audience at a CIPD conference (85% women) when the male presenter used a poor metaphor to describe the difference between intrinsic and extrinsic rewards, using the old line that payment for doing good work (extrinsic reward) was the equivalent of 'all fur coat and no knickers'. He thought it was hilarious. The audience didn't. There's a thin line between grabbing attention for the right and the wrong reasons. That's why using humour is scary for many presenters.

Oops! Fall from Grace

And that's exactly what happened to me during a recent pitch – this time (again) to a group of nurses. In fact, I may have had a double whammy in that neither the content nor the style of the presentation went down well and the feedback was suitably brutal (I brought along a guy to play a piece of music and they seemed to like him – so that's something to cling to). In this particular case, I'd made the rookie error of not doing enough research on the exact needs of the audience and ran a 'pitch' for a more advanced group that completely missed the mark. *Lesson #1*: You have to do your homework – and I screwed up.

Public speaking is not for the faint-hearted. And, no matter how experienced we are, from time to time we all make mistakes and fall from grace. But, here's the kicker. **It's almost impossible to**

build a successful executive career without being a reasonably good public speaker. You don't have to morph into Barack Obama. And you don't have to 'win' every single pitch you make. But, if you are ambitious, you can't avoid this area. If you are not 'cured' already, I suggest you undertake a public speaking course – something tough (if it doesn't challenge you, it probably won't change you either). In addition to honing your speaking skills, the ability to make great presentations builds confidence. So that's the *pitch* this week. Now, you just need to get cracking on it!

ELIMINATE THE MOST COMMON MISTAKES IN BUSINESS WRITING

One of the daily newspapers recently ran a competition for a short story that had to be completed in six words or less. No doubt the idea was inspired by Ernest Hemingway, who penned the following gem:

Fire Sale. Baby's shoes. Never used.

While few can aspire to Hemingway's genius, we can set our sights a bit lower and still write really well. So, here's the question: Are you a good writer?

In my opinion, writing is a hugely important part of the executive toolkit and you need to get good at this. Take this quick test:

Positive Indicators (pat yourself on the back)

♦ You enjoy writing and can pull your thoughts together quickly.

♦ You read a lot of books, including novels (increases vocabulary).

♦ It's easy for you to find words to express what you mean.

Contra-indicators (start worrying)

♦ You dislike writing and avoid it where possible.

- It takes you a long time to capture what you want to say.
- You can bang off an email, but longer reports / analyses are difficult to construct.

Becoming a Great Writer

One approach is simply to eliminate the typical 'mistakes' that people make when writing even simple emails. You ignore the following points at your peril:

- **Albert Reynolds:** Writers often overestimate the amount of information that the human brain can process. Keep it *simple* (use short words and short sentences) and keep it *single* (one purpose). Think of your reader as 'Albert Reynolds' (the former Taoiseach would not accept any briefing that was longer than one page).

- **Too much:** Who wants to read a 3,168-word email? Perhaps it is more a 'CYA' for the sender than a message to the receiver? *Key point:* responsibility for effective communications stays with the sender. That responsibility doesn't end when you press the 'send' button. It's up to you to ensure that your message gets through. In writing, less is more.

- **Too soon:** I had one colleague who liked to send 'draft' materials. He drove me nuts with 'stream of consciousness' stuff that had not been thought through, structured or edited. But he felt good that it was 'done', one more thing off his 'To Do' list. That's like throwing a pile of logs on the ground and thinking that it will assemble itself into a table. Unless you are in the Pentagon, most things don't have to be sent immediately. Draft it. Then correct it. Right doesn't mean 'right now' and most writing is re-writing!

- **So what?** Let's assume that you have described the situation in clear language and people understand the core point. So what? What do you want the reader to do? (for example, torture the CEO, make a €1 million donation to Amnesty International, fly to Australia to sort out a massive koala bear infestation?). Make your 'ask' crystal clear.

From Great To Inspired

Now, let's assume that you have mastered the basics and want to step it up a gear. You don't want to be a *good* writer; you want to be a *great* writer. What should you do next? There are a couple of possibilities to hone your art. You could:

- **Analyse your current writing:** Ask a journalist or a professional writer to look at examples you've completed. Do you have a 'style' that is powerful and persuasive?

- **Join a Writers Group:** There are a lot of writers groups around (mostly focused on fiction; it might help with the annual report!). While you may not wish to become a candidate for the Booker Prize, some of the 'tricks' learned can be applied in your day job.

- **Be reader-focused:** The central principle here = identification, getting into the hearts and minds of your audience. Remind yourself of the American Indian maxim: "To understand another, it is necessary to walk in his moccasins". Recall a personal contact with the person you are writing to. Relate recent events to the group that will interest them. Use logic and emotion to get inside their guard and lift the communication beyond the mundane.

Good News

Most business writing is boring and you won't have to do much to appear smart in this space. I could say more but this bloody quill keeps breaking and it took so long to catch that last Golden Eagle and to pluck it!

Section 4:

PERSONAL
EFFECTIVENESS

USING MEETING TIME PRODUCTIVELY

OK, OK, you've heard all the jokes before. Meetings are places where you keep minutes and lose hours. Meetings are… (add your own tag lines). I've just spent four hours writing an agenda for a meeting. During the four hours, I made a cup of tea, so it was probably only three hours and 55 minutes. The agenda was for a two-day meeting, with six key discussion items, and ended up as a two-page document. Was this an agenda or a 'short story' I hear you ask? Let's take a quick journey backwards in time to explain.

Great Weddings

Over the past number of years, I've been to a couple of brilliant weddings. In a big family, there is always some nephew or niece getting hitched (someone said to me recently that they'd rather get a speeding ticket in the post than a wedding invitation – it costs less!). Now, here's the sure-fire formula for success. Weddings that work really well have been planned in advance. The band was checked out a year earlier. The couple ate at the hotel, anonymously, to see if the food was good. And so on. You can't fully plan for your Uncle Larry making a pass at the bridesmaid(s), but you can usually make sure that the church service goes well. And you can ensure that two maiden aunts who haven't spoken since 1971 are not sitting at the same table (throw a half bottle of vodka into that mix and the involvement of the riot police is practically guaranteed). In similar vein, great meetings are equally well planned.

Setting Agendas

I've been a participant in meetings that ranged from the boring (with people falling asleep) to the bizarre ("Anyone for a game of Jenga to get the creativity flowing?"). This last example was at a meeting called to discuss headcount reductions.

It's important to get meetings off to a great start. Like 100-metre Olympics sprinters, you need to understand your strategy before the race starts, not 'recover' during the meeting. The key to this is setting out the agenda very strongly. If you write an agenda cryptically with headings like 'cost' or 'quality', no one has any idea what's meant by this or what you are actually going to discuss. Elaborating – for example, *Cost: Can we reduce the current expenditure from 14% of costs of goods sold to under 10%?* – helps the focus enormously.

The Building Blocks

Meetings are a key building block in most organisations. Well-run sessions (clear agendas and good chairmanship) overcome confusion, set a positive tone (solid groundrules for behaviour) and are respectful of people's time (staying on track; confusing or contentious items get bottomed out). To help him organise better meetings, one client asked me to develop a 'best-practice checklist'. The outcome is reproduced below. Use this template when you're planning your next session.

1: Preparation for Meetings

 ◆ Why have a meeting anyway? What are we trying to achieve?

- Would an email / informal discussion suffice?
- Who should be invited? What's the optimum number? Does everyone have to be present?
- Do you need to 'sell' any ideas in advance of the meeting, or explain your strategy to key individuals?
- What exactly do you want to achieve? Is it a problem-solving meeting, a bargaining meeting, etc?
- What location would best suit the purpose? How should the room be set out to achieve this?
- Distribute the agenda in advance of the meeting.

2: Writing the Agenda

- Don't skimp on the wording. Make each section crystal clear.
- Label each agenda item (for info, for discussion, for decision).
- Items that will 'unify' the group should be near the top of the agenda.
- Items that need high mental energy should be near the top of the agenda.
- Put finishing times on each agenda item and try to stick to them.
- Keep the agenda manageable in size. Sometimes 'less is more.'
- Plan start times to keep the meeting short (for example, start an hour before lunch / quitting time).

3: Role of the Chairperson

- Start the meeting on time. Don't penalise those who come early by delaying.

- Agree the objectives of the meeting with the group.

- Groundrules: Agree (if not already done) the decision-making process, who will keep notes, etc.

- Be aware of the three dimensions of a meeting (achieving the *Task*, managing the *Process*, acknowledging people's *Feelings*). A good chairperson works on all three levels.

- Keep the meeting on track. Move the discussion forward when points have been agreed or where further information is necessary.

- Use 'interim summaries' to give the group a feeling of accomplishment.

- Control any long-winded people: "Thanks Tom, I understand you've made your feelings known on that topic" or "Let's get everyone in on this".

- Keep your antenna alert. "What's happening in the group that's unspoken?"

- Hidden agendas? Are some people taking a position as 'delegates' / protecting their patch / group? If so, should you confront it, suppress it or encourage it to be brought into the open?

- In longer meetings, consider a 'half time' question: "Are we getting what we want from this meeting?"

4: Ensuring Good Discussion of ideas

- Introduce each item and clarify the discussion to prevent misunderstanding or confusion.

- Does the group have a solid diagnosis (of the exact problem, on the required solution)?

- Encourage clash of ideas / discourage clash of personalities.

- Don't dominate the discussion. Use the full resources of the group.
- Draw out silent members. Don't mistake silence for agreement. Everyone is part of the show.
- Don't allow 'new' ideas or suggestions to get squashed at birth. Encourage / build on them.
- Continually test for understanding and commitment. Use active listening techniques.

5: Bringing to Conclusion

- Summarise what has been agreed.
- Re-test for commitment on any contentious items. When taking 'straw polls', ask the most senior people last.
- Avoid glossing over disagreements. Put unfinished business in the context of what has been agreed.
- Close on a note of achievement.

6: Following a Meeting

- Issue minutes containing: Time / date; names of those present / absent; acknowledgement of items discussed / decisions made; reconfirmation of date / time / place for next meeting.

You can see from this checklist why a lot of meetings don't work well. Perhaps **the ideal is to have fewer actual meetings but ensure the ones you attend are fully productive**. Sometimes, the very best ideas are simple.

TIME MANAGEMENT:
HOW TO MASTER YOUR DIARY

The secret to time management is simple. Do your important work first and ignore everything else. Here's an example from the military…

The Duke of Wellington, during the Peninsular Campaign, wrote to the British Foreign Office in London as follows:

> We have enumerated our saddles, bridles, tents and tent poles, and all manner of sundry items for which his Majesty's Government holds me accountable. Unfortunately, the sum of one shilling and nine pence remains unaccounted for in one infantry battalion's petty cash and there has been a hideous confusion as to the number of jars of raspberry jam issued to one cavalry regiment … This brings me to my present purpose, which is to request elucidation of my instructions. Is it (1) to train an army of uniformed British clerks in Spain for the benefit of the accounting and copy boys in London, or, perchance (2) to see to it that the forces of Napoleon are driven out of Spain?"

To master your time, you need to systematically focus on importance, not urgency. As humans, we are pre-wired to focus on things that demand an immediate response (for example, email alerts). But, if the cost of this is to postpone things that are important, it's a heavy price to pay for perceived efficiency. You need to reverse that order and learn to systematically work on what's important. Here's how to do this…

Principle 1: Set Clear Objectives

Most people need to figure out four to seven key objectives they have for the year. These objectives have different 'labels' in different organisations – but the principle is exactly the same. What are the key things that I will produce this year?

The 'trick' here is to understand the difference between inputs and outputs. An old joke may help to explain. Two sales representatives were talking in Cork. One said: "I made a lot of strategic contacts today". His friend replied: "Yeah, I didn't get any sales either". Outputs are end results that pay the bills. Inputs are activities, that don't necessarily produce anything positive.

Some people get caught up with these 'busyness' indicators that don't actually move the needle forward. I recently worked with a senior executive in a technology company. He received more than 500 emails a day. Now, unless you have an objective titled 'Keeping my Inbox' clear, this level of 'noise' is just a distraction. The central issue here = focus. Focusing on one task at a time is normally more efficient than multi-tasking and gives you the opportunity to excel (now guys, you don't need to feel guilty about not being able to multi-task).

Principle 2: First Things First

What is the single most important (not urgent) thing you could possibly be doing? Customer service? Staff relations? Business process re-engineering? Revenue growth? Do some of that today. Remember there are a limitless number of distractions – don't fool yourself by thinking "If I just do this thing, then I will…".

People have a gravitational pull towards what they know, what they like and what they feel comfortable doing. A couple of years back, I met the site manager of a pharmaceutical plant to talk about strategic planning. When I arrived, his PA told me that he was 'in the factory'. Turns out that he was physically repairing a tablet press, the machine that forms the shape of tablets. Why? He was an engineer. His first love was machines. Talking to me about strategic planning was well down his list of 'want to do' stuff. *The problem:* Planning was a key part of his job and he was essentially running away from it. Perhaps at home you can continually 'postpone' cutting the grass or painting the shed – but, in work, you have to tackle critical issues right away, so quit stalling!

Principle 3: Work Your Diary

Some people are morning grouches but can work till midnight. Others are 'larks' and get their best work done early in the day. You have to know your own body clock. Schedule time in your diary to do your most important work – and don't be at everyone else's beck and call. Personally, I like tackling tough jobs in the morning and leaving the afternoon free for 'easy stuff' like chatting to people, returning phone calls, messing with emails and so on. You need to find your own *modus operandi*.

There are two sub-points here worth making:

♦ **Kill updates:** Technology has evolved to exploit our urgency addiction: email, Facebook, Quora (and more) will fight to distract you constantly. Fortunately, this is easily fixed. Turn off all notifications or choose to check these things when you have time to be distracted – say, during a lunch break – and work through them together, saving time. Here's the BIG news. You are in charge (not your computer or phone). I decided to exit Twitter when I read the following tweet: "Had a great shower this morning. What a way to start the day". There is some stuff you just don't need to know. Overcome your FOMO (Fear Of Missing Out anxiety) and get on with your real job. Ryan Tubridy bailed out of Twitter because of the level of personal abuse he was getting. Those Internet trolls might have, inadvertently, done him a favour – making him much more productive. Get rid of the noise in your life!

♦ **Schedule priorities:** If you have a friend to meet, you'll arrange to see them at a set time. But if you have something that matters to you more than anything – say writing a book, or going to the gym – many people don't schedule it. They feel that they will somehow just 'get around to it'. Treat your highest priorities like flights you have to catch: give them a set time in advance and say "No" to anything that would stop you making your flight. Is it a bit robotic? Absolutely. And what's wrong with that? (within reason). Welcome to the world of *über*-efficiency. The old 'To Do' list (whether electronic or paper version) still has a role to play

Principle 4: Learn to Say "No"

Most of us follow an implicit social contract: when someone asks us to do something, we almost always want to say "Yes" – perhaps just because you were asked nicely! Although it may feel noble to say "Yes", while you are in 'response mode' your own work may not be getting done. You may need to sacrifice some social comfort to get your own stuff done (as a bonus, people tend to instinctively respect those who can say "No").

Part of saying "No" (in a silent way) is to ignore some requests. It might seem rude, unprofessional. But often, it's absolutely necessary. There are people you won't find time to reply to. There are requests you will allow yourself to forget. You can be slow to do things like tidying up, paying bills or opening mail. The world won't fall apart. The payoff is you get things done that matter. You don't have to be a jerk – but you do have to learn how to say "No". Let people 'keep their own monkeys' – it's not your mission to 'save the world' (unless you are thinking of kicking off a new religion).

Principle 5: Handle Each Piece of Paper Once

Procrastinators are time-wasters (sometimes, they suffer from perfectionism). They choose something on the desk to look at. If it's concerning or confusing or both, they say "Oh shit" before putting it back into the pile. They constantly move stuff 'around' their desk or keep updating 'To Do' lists – providing the illusion of progress. When you take up a task (assuming it's a priority task), the key is to move it forward. Decide to do something about it. Sometimes, the 'Swiss cheese principle' needs to be deployed (when you 'put holes' in a big job until it eventually collapses) – but most of the time small tasks need to be completed there and then. Pick it up. Make the call. Complete the step. Move on. Sometimes, 90% now beats 100% never!

By following the five principles outlined above, you can learn to become productive and give yourself an extra couple of hours each week. That's a full round of golf, or three Shazam classes in the gym. Look, if worse comes to worst, you could even spend extra time with the family. Now, there's a thought…

PRIORITISATION: HOW DOING LESS OFTEN DELIVERS MORE

I recently spoke to a senior banking executive. He wasn't bored. Among a plethora of tasks he faced, he was looking at ways to re-engage with staff, re-structure the organisation, figure out how to make hundreds of people redundant with dignity while, at the same time, developing better internal risk management processes. Phew! I was tired just listening to his agenda.

Work Longer

When senior executives are faced with an overwhelming agenda, what do they do? Well, it depends. In a business that is growing, they have the option of hiring more staff or using consultants as an extra pair of hands to 'shore up the ship'. But, in a loss-making business, they are usually constrained. There's often no money and even less tolerance for additional spending. This can be coupled with a negative vibe ("You got us into this mess, so figure the way out"). Faced with the above, most executives work harder. Punch in longer hours. Attend more meetings. Get stuck into the detail and lead from the front. Despite the best intentions, it's usually a mistake.

The Battleship

In the military world, a battleship is for the protection of other ships. Now, the first three duties of a battleship are

♦ To stay afloat.

♦ To stay afloat.

♦ To stay afloat.

If you are not afloat yourself, you cannot protect anyone else. When you are 'running on empty', you become cranky, half-listening, joyless. You become a 'long hours machine' (measuring inputs) and stop being an effective executive (producing outputs).

Top Three

You need to prioritise. Call a halt to your Mother Teresa impersonation (a bit non-PC, but very descriptive – John Randles uses the phrase: "Get down off your cross").

Identify your top three or four critical tasks. Stay focused on these – like a bee tracking the scent of a flower. And don't try to satisfy other people's needs in the organisation while you are doing this. People own their own happiness. Your job is to stabilise the organisation and, in the words of Tom Peters, "keep the herd moving roughly west".

Prioritisation delivers results. Try it.

Section 5:

CHANGE
MANAGEMENT

READY, STEADY – DON'T GO! PLANNING IS KEY TO SUCCESS

I'm not usually BIG on heroes, but I really admire Rory McIlroy. He has (hopefully) a long career ahead. It's hard not to be proud of the fact that this tiny island has produced so many excellent golfers. We can 'almost' claim the world number 1 spot. Sports fans and Gerry Adams have one thing in common; we all want to get rid of that border!

Brilliant Planning

There was a report on the radio highlighting the fact that Rory's former home (30 minutes from Belfast) was available for rent. You could stay there for a week (a snip @ £12,000) or visit on a day trip. The house has an attached golf course with some unusual features. It contains different types of grasses from golf courses around the world - allowing you to practice on the different surfaces. It also has a range of imported sand in the bunkers - representing variations used on golf courses across the globe. With this level of preparation, is it any wonder that the man is world-class? Now, stay with me for a moment as we gravitate towards what might euphemistically be termed lower-end planning.

A Proper Gig

We were asked to play a music gig in north county Dublin – I can't name the venue for fear of years of litigation. We put together an improvised set list and 'rehearsed' for about an hour. Hey, we're all busy and it's not the day job. Right?

On the night, one member of the band was definitely 'worse for wear'. He kept confusing chords, playing in the wrong key and singing the first verse of each song seven times. We were using a new PA system, which didn't have enough inputs. I'd brought along a separate amplifier that couldn't be heard – other than as some form of 'noise competition' with the larger PA. The 'sound' problems got to me and my own effort on the night was just brutal. But there was hope!

Unusually, Linda had come to the gig with her buddy Margaret. They sauntered up to the stage at the break. That's the exact moment when you need a bit of comfort from your partner, TLC to boost a flagging confidence. What Linda actually said was: "Jesus, you are shite". Earlier in the evening, we'd had a spat so perhaps this was *payback*. She's actually suggested that a good movie title for her own life would be *30 Years a Slave!*

Quick Rescue

During the break, a young guy in the audience (who I knew from previous gigs) asked if he could play a few tunes. I set him up and encouraged a couple of his mates to take up the role of 'backing singers'. They bought into it and the crowd loved it. We also recruited a woman who we heard could play guitar and sing solo. A bit of a risk, as we'd never met before. She was inspired. Brilliant. Turned the whole event around. We came back on stage and managed to close it out well. Overall, the night ended up on the plus side. In reality, we 'got away with it'. Just don't tell anyone.

So What?

What has all of the above got to do with you? Well, think of Rory McIlroy practising on that sand from Dubai. And think about our band, with the equivalent of 5% of his natural talent, 'showing up' and hoping that everything would be grand on the night.

In terms of preparing for big 'events', are you closer to the Rory model or the bad wedding band? In every executive role, there are a couple of key events each year. Perhaps three to five. In terms of these, **you need to plan your success in advance rather than leaving it to chance** – regardless of how talented you are. Planning and rehearsing entails working late or through the weekend. Not all the time – but definitely for those important 'gigs'. Whatever it takes to nail it.

For sure, not everything can be pre-planned. There are times when we all have to manage on instinct and cope with the unexpected. During a recent radio interview I was asked, completely off-topic, about the links between psychopaths and CEOs and how many psychopaths I'd personally met who were in the CEO chair (I couldn't immediately think of anyone I wanted to name on national radio; perhaps in a future blog?).

Yes, hang onto your spontaneity. But being great on your feet is not mutually exclusive from planning. As Abraham Lincoln said:

> *Give me six hours to chop down a tree and I will spend the first four sharpening the axe.*

Careers are made and lost on big events. Don't let them slip by you for the want of a drop of planning.

IMPROVE YOUR PERFORMANCE BY NARROWING YOUR GOALS: HOW TO STAY FOCUSED

Let me start with a *confession*: I don't really know anything about politics. Yes, I religiously follow all the political spats in the media. And, I've been in the Dáil on a variety of missions. But, overall, I know as much about politics as Ivor Callely appears to know about estimating the distance from Clontarf to Kildare Street (it's about 380 kilometres, right?).

Political Contact

That's why I was surprised when the contact came. A budding politician – seeking election in Dublin – wanted someone to manage the campaign. Was I interested? I was intrigued enough to go along to the meeting. This woman, whom I instantly liked, had spent most of her life on the fringes of politics. It was now time to move out of the shadows and make a real play for a Dáil seat. *The Question:* Could I help her craft a winning election strategy?

I deployed the *Manuel Defence* ("I know nothing") but she didn't seem to be put off. So, we decided to do a 'mini-election-strategy' session there and then in the restaurant. It made a change from discussing Ireland's 'eight-month-long winters'. The conversation ran along the following lines:

> *"What sort of issues will you campaign on?"*
>
> *"That's not the way it works. The electorate decide the issues and I represent them."*
>
> *"Talk me through that?"*
>
> *"Well, you thoroughly canvass the area. Then you group the data that people have raised and categorise it."*
>
> *"OK. What sort of issues are important in your area?"* (a mix of Dublin City Council and middle class housing).
>
> *"Well, there are tons of issues. Crime and fear of crime is a hot topic. Of course, there's always economics – zero jobs and high taxes. Then there are working mothers; a lack of provision of crèche places along with the general cost of childcare. There are also some environmental concerns around the proposed*

*construction of an incinerator. There's a heap of stuff
emerging around the reform of politics itself, how
expenses are recorded and all that".*

*"It's a long list. What do you see as your particular
'calling card?' What will you focus on?*

*"I don't think you understood the original point.
Politicians don't decide the issues, the electorate
decides".*

*"Where do you see yourself having a particular
interest? Where is your own passion?"*

*(Getting somewhat agitated now). "I keep telling you. I
will follow the electorate, not push them down
avenues that are pet topics for me. Are you hearing
the message?"*

"OK, I have it."

"You have what?"

*"I've figured out your campaign slogan. It's really
memorable."*

"Jesus, that was quick. Go on, what is it?"

"Vote for me. I will improve absolutely everything."

Not Funny

She didn't think that was particularly funny. Neither did I. I told her
that politicians need to take a stance on issues. It's called
branding. Think Ming Flanagan in his heyday (allowing people
access to cutting turf – despite EU regulations making it illegal).
She understood the point – but felt that you couldn't narrow down
to a handful of issues. There were 100+ issues in the constituency
and she would provide a platform for all 100+ views. I thought her

proposed strategy was nuts and we parted amicably. I'm not sure who eventually helped her with the campaign, but she didn't get elected (in fairness, she was running against some very seasoned players).

Banking Executive

I had a somewhat similar experience in one of the main banks. (Like President Clinton daydreaming about the 1980s, let me inhale a moment of nostalgia here. Oh yes, the good old days when the banks used consultants.) An executive was promoted into a role where he didn't have a lot of experience and I was asked to coach him, specifically to co-author his objectives for the coming year. I asked about his legacy, what he hoped to achieve over the next three years (the average lifespan for an executive in that bank to remain in a single role). He said: "Can we skip the philosophy lesson and get on with setting the objectives?" But you can't just roll over at the first sign of opposition, so I stuck to the point.

His Legacy

I asked him how he would like to be remembered. Did he want to be 'Mr Top Line' – the man who had improved revenue flows (there were a number of possible M&A options)? Or did he want to be 'Mr Bottom Line' – using business process reengineering to rip out every non-value-added step in a slimmed-down organisation? Perhaps he wanted to be 'Mr Customer Service' – improving the Net Promoter Score? As a final twist, he could become 'Mr Staff Engagement' – making sure that the group managed (about 2,800 people) were in fifth gear, happier than a group of alcoholics on a guided tour of the Jameson Distillery. The only answer disallowed was: "I want to be remembered for all of the above" because some of these ideas are mutually exclusive.

As soon as he decided his intended legacy, I would work backwards from it and clinically set out what he needed to achieve in the next 12 months. As a final kicker, I reminded him of the Einstein quote:

Intellectuals solve problems; geniuses prevent them.

Stay Focused

Lots of us behave like that budding politician and the banking executive. In trying to appeal to 'everyone', we run the risk of appealing to no one. We'd do well to remember the Chinese proverb:

When you chase two rabbits, you catch neither.

The suggestion is as follows: Fold up that superhero cape. Consider what you can actually achieve in your time in the chair. Yes, Earthling, focus on human scale stuff. And then actually deliver it. Move out of the land of dreaming and into the land of doing. Because results pay the bills. **You are paid to get things done, not to go home tired**. Being *focused* is the engine of performance improvement. Simple, isn't it?

THOSE DAMN BEHAVIOURS ARE HARD TO SHIFT ... PERHAPS YOU ARE IMMUNE TO CHANGE?

The Holy Grail for consultants is to understand change – how organisations and individuals make progress. While most consultants are happy to chat freely about success stories, poster boys and girls who've successfully made the journey, they may be reluctant to highlight cases where progress has been less than stellar. Because the reality is that some clients get 'stuck'. God, if only someone would write a book and decipher all this complex psychology stuff. Well, now that you mention it... the book *Immunity to Change,* written by Professor Robert Kegan and Lisa Lahey of Harvard University, covers this topic. It's hard to do justice to their thesis in a short piece, but here's the skinny.

Change is Difficult

To illustrate the point that people find it difficult to make behavioural changes, they cite the example of medical patients. Picture the scene. You've been told to take a particular medicine to prevent you from having a stroke and dying. That seems like a pretty good motivation. Add in the idea of zero cost (the medicine is covered by your health insurance company) and there are no side effects. Whoopee! A no-brainer; gimme that pill. But studies in the USA demonstrate, time after time, that a high percentage of the population in this situation stop taking vital medicines. **One estimate in the USA put the percentage long-term**

compliance at just 54%. So, what's going on here. Why are intelligent people doing stupid things (or, more correctly, not doing clever things)?

Immunity to Change

The book sets out to answer that question. To cut to the chase, there are often forces – things outside of our conscious unawareness – that sabotage behaviour. If you don't uncover and understand these factors, you don't make progress – nothing changes.

Let's use a less dramatic example than someone dying of a stroke. Think of administering a 360-degree feedback instrument. When the person receives the feedback, sometimes the response is: "There's nothing really new here. I knew this stuff already". Isn't it hard to restrain yourself from saying: "And if you knew this already, how come it's still on the shit list?"

How Does It Work?

Immunity to change is based on the fundamental idea that 'not changing' is actually an anxiety management system. The analogy of an 'immune' system was chosen because this protects the body from disease. In similar vein, a 'mental immunity' protects the person from anxiety – working in the background and automatically keeping us 'safe'.

The good news is that we don't become overwhelmed by anxiety. If I hate conflict and shy away from it, I am 'protected' from the anxiety which this generates.

The bad news? It creates a false belief that certain things are impossible. For example, if I avoid conflict all the time (because this makes me anxious and I have 'self-protected'), then there are situations where I am limited as an executive or in my personal life. Because there are times when 'conflict' is exactly what's needed to move the needle forward (I'm not revealing anything about Linda dropping that sofa on my foot in 1997; my lips are sealed).

Learning provides another good example. When I learn something new (to drive a car or write computer code), it makes me feel anxious. I feel a bit stupid when material is hard to grasp or when I can't perform some motor function. So, should I stop learning in order to avoid the anxiety that this provokes? Hardly. But that's exactly what some people do. They stop growing in order to avoid anxiety. And the killer part is that a lot of this 'avoidance' happens subconsciously – below our level of awareness. It's like a governor being placed on your car accelerator, limiting the speed at which you can travel, without anyone telling you this. This 'mental governor' limits the speed at which we develop and grow as a person.

The Fix

So, what's the solution? Well the first step is to become aware of this issue. You 'peel away the layers' of this onion and get to the core. The methodology is not straightforward to explain.

First, you pick 'one big thing' that you are going to change in your life' (something important that would really make a difference). You then create a sort of X-ray to understand why you are not changing this, listing all the things you are doing or not doing that actually work against your goal. The third step is to reveal your 'worry box' (hidden competing commitments that you feel will happen if you did change). *Example:* In the case of the 'non-taking' of stroke medicine, a common underlying concern was that people felt "taking medicine daily was the behaviour of old men" (**to avoid looking like 'old men', they behaved in a way that ensured they would soon become dead men**). I know, I know. Outwardly, this seems ridiculous – but these are not rational processes that can be held up to the light. The final step is to figure out the core assumptions – hidden beliefs that make sense of this type of behaviour. By reviewing the 'completed map', you make sense of it all.

Unlimited Possibility

The core idea is to 'remove the unconscious ceiling' that may have been holding you back from reaching your potential. Those assumptions – like an electric fence marking out forbidden territory – could be making you 'immune to change'. It sounds a bit complex but my personal take on this is that it's well worth the effort.

Let's leave the last word to Professor Kegan:

> *If 14 frogs sat on a log and 3 decided to jump into the lake, how many would be left?*
>
> *You're probably thinking 11.*
>
> *But the answer might be 14. There is a big difference between desire and action.*

Now, go jump in a lake!

PERSONAL BRANDING: 12 PHOTO TYPES YOU DON'T WANT TO USE ON YOUR PROFILE

I'm amazed at the photos that people use as part of their LinkedIn profile – with little thought about the impact these might have on the viewing public!

How does that work? You go to a huge amount of bother to set up your profile, pulling together all the good bits from academic and work records. *Goal:* Make the reader believe that you can turnaround failing economies, anticipate the emergence of entire new industries and rescue animals from burning buildings. Then, when that's done, you simply 'paste in' whatever photo happens to be to hand. (Those of us who are less photogenic are more attuned to the need for a half-decent mug shot.)

So, without further ado and without offering even a scintilla of supporting scientific evidence to back this up, here's a jaundiced view of how your photo might be seen by others:

- **Wearing sunglasses** (or sunglasses placed on head): *Message:* "Yes, I'm cool. I've visited places in the world where the sun breaks through the cloud cover and where sunglasses are more than a fashion item". *Suggestion:* Lose the accessories.

- **Speaking into a microphone:** Well now, look at you! Who's a clever boy? So clever, in fact, that people want to *amplify* what you say – without missing a single word. *Suggestion:* Unless you are auditioning for a non-speaking role, people will assume that you can talk. Ditch the mic.

- **Graduation Ball:** These photos come complete with bow tie / elegant evening dress (delete as appropriate; the two don't really go well together). *Message:* "Don't I look fabulous?" No, you look like someone trying to appear fully-grown up. *Suggestion:* Kit yourself out in some actual work attire. We know that you went to college. Congratulations. Now, let it go...

- **Cartoon photo:** Have you seen these cartoon representations? Mostly used by *creative* types in the marketing world. *Message:* Any gobshite can get a headshot, but it takes real talent to source something as cool as this. Black and white cartoons are a variation, telling the world that you are retro cool. It's up there with skateboarding to work. But... it creates a tiny nagging doubt that you are trying a 'bit too hard'? Perhaps I'm wrestling with my own unconscious jealousy that I couldn't pull off that 'look'.

- **Outdoor pursuits:** This is the unexpected 'shot' taken while you are wearing a mountain climbing harness against a gargantuan cliff backdrop (substitute kite surfing or deep sea diving while feeding a school of man-eating sharks). *Message:* "I am particularly interesting and *virile* (The guilty party? Mainly men! Women have more sense – or do they? See next category). Hire me and you won't just meet a programmer (they always seem to be 'techies') but you will get to know a 'rounded person' who has no limits". *Unspoken:* "I know that LinkedIn is for business and is not a dating website, but nothing wrong with an each-way bet, is there?" *The viewer's take:* He couldn't be bothered to find a more normal photo because he probably doesn't comply with 'organisation rules' and thinks it's all crap. This category overlaps with the **exotic location** photograph. *Message:* "Hello there! Greetings from... wherever. That's me with the Taj Mahal / Eiffel Tower / Mount Fuji just slightly out of focus in the background. Don't think of me as just an Irishman or even a European. I'm more a citizen of the world. If you want to book me on a Ryanair flight to Birmingham to do great strategic work, I'm up for it. Because, I've been on planes before and didn't pick up beriberi (it was just a mild flu)". *Good News:* Don't worry, it's not incurable. You will (hopefully) eventually grow out of the juvenile habit of boasting about where you've been. Removing that stupid photo is the first step.

♦ **Mad Maxine:** Look into my eyes. Am I not the living, breathing, and spitting image of Kung Fu Panda? You can't fool me. *Everyone* loved that movie". Some of these photos look like a team from the Brown Thomas make-up counter worked on the candidate, non-stop, for 72 hours. *Message:* "I'm sophisticated". Eh, no you're not actually. You look like someone trying to look 27 years older. *Suggestion:* Lose the OTT look; you don't need it.

♦ **Very serious face:** Message: "This is I. I'm solid, semi-intellectual and WYSIWYG". Quite. But we're not convinced that we want to chat to someone in the canteen who looks like they've been constipated for the entire month of March. Lighten up. Jesus, did you just take one photograph? Who stole all the smiley ones?

♦ **Head resting on hands:** The photo can be full-face or a softer 'profile' shot – but they always have the candidate staring intently into the camera while resting their chin on one hand. *Message:* "This is me in a thoughtful pose. I am confident, have hidden depth and an awful lot to offer". *Actual impact:* Are those stupid poses still in vogue? I thought this stuff was canned in the 1960s? Sack the photographer!

- **No photo:** Somewhat intriguing. The viewer is torn between two contradictory ideas: *#1:* This person is an independent thinker. S/he does not just 'comply' with the instruction to post a photo. Perhaps a bit of a rebel – but in an understated way. Certainly worth meeting, if only to satisfy a curiosity. *#2:* This person is either too lazy to put up a photo or couldn't figure out how to do it. Perhaps a radical feminist who refuses to put age or marital status on her CV. A bit risky?

- **Uncontrollable laughing:** This one has a bit of *form* – for example, the Dutch painter Frans Hals finished working on 'The Laughing Cavalier' in 1624. *Message:* "Your search is at an end. I am the very man / women that you urgently need to hire for the sports and social committee. As a bonus, I do a terrific karaoke impression of Right Said Fred singing *I'm too sexy for my shirt*". *Suggestion:* While such entertainment skills are undoubtedly useful in times of acute stress (during a nuclear war), perhaps you shouldn't lead with this as your 'trump card' in peacetime?

- **Wearing headphones:** A (surprisingly) common photo. Couple of possible subliminal messages at play here. Choose from one of the following options: (a) "I am a man but capable of multi-tasking – for example, listening to music while stabbing my index finger at the keyboard"; (b) "I am über-cool. Check out the way my headphones colour coordinate with my vest"; (c) "I'm actually very wealthy. You don't want to know how much these Beats noise cancellation headphones knocked me back. Well actually, now that you have mentioned it, they cost me over €400 in a closing down sale where I managed to snag the last pair. I only do quality – because that's who I am". *Suggestion:* Lose the headphones. Fast.

- **With partner / child:** Message: "Look at me, *please*. Here's photographic evidence (completely free from any form of digital manipulation) that someone loves and needs me deeply. Can't you see how *close* we are? My charisma is practically leaping off the page. *Isn't it?* I'm great with other people, a natural. That's exactly the sort of team player you're looking for. *Right*?" Eh, actually no, it isn't. We were trying to hire an individual with key skills, not create a relationship with your extended family. Next!

So, there you have it. A guide to the impact of photo profiles on LinkedIn. Think about how your photo can positively or negatively affect your 'personal branding'. What message is your current photo communicating about you? It's not just consultants who are in the sales business...

Disclaimer

No actual LinkedIn users were hurt during the construction of this blog. If you have been affected by anything contained here, dial 1-800-I-Need A-New-Photo. Out-of-work press photographers can usually be sourced on any evening after 8.30 in Mulligan's pub in Poolbeg Street, Dublin. They have been drinking there, steadily, since the *Irish Press* offices closed down in 1995. Just buy the first round and you could end up with a terrific head and shoulders portrait that makes you look like George Clooney.

PAUL MOONEY

Paul Mooney holds a Ph.D. and a Post-Graduate Diploma in Industrial Sociology (Trinity College). He also holds an M.Sc. and a Post-Graduate Diploma in Advanced Executive & Business Coaching (University College Dublin), along with a National Diploma in Industrial Relations (National College of Ireland). Paul is a Fellow of the Chartered Institute of Personnel & Development and is widely recognised as an expert on organisation and individual change.

Paul began his working life as a butcher in Dublin. After completing a formal apprenticeship, he moved into production management. He subsequently joined General Electric and held a number of human resource positions in manufacturing. After

GE, Paul worked with Sterling Drug in Ireland and the Pacific Rim, with responsibility for all HR activity across Asia.

On return to Ireland, he established a management consulting company specialising in Organisation and Management Development. Between 2007 and 2010, Paul held the position of President, National College of Ireland. He subsequently set up Tandem Consulting, a team of senior OD / Change specialists. Tandem's client list reads like a 'Who's Who' of Irish and multinational organisations with consulting assignments across 20+ countries – for both public and private sector clients.

Paul is the author of 14 books covering a wide span of issues and topics around organisation performance and personal change. Areas of expertise include:

- ◆ Organisational Development / Change and Conflict Resolution.
- ◆ Leadership Development / Executive Coaching.
- ◆ Human Resource Management / Employee Engagement.

His blog *'Confessions of a Consultant'* can be sourced at **http://tandemconsulting.wordpress.com**.

OAK TREE PRESS

Oak Tree Press develops and delivers information, advice and resources for entrepreneurs and managers. It is Ireland's leading business book publisher, with an unrivalled reputation for quality titles across business, management, HR, law, marketing and enterprise topics.

In addition, Oak Tree Press occupies a unique position in start-up and small business support in Ireland through its standard-setting titles, as well training courses, mentoring and advisory services.

Oak Tree Press is comfortable across a range of communication media – print, web and training, focusing always on the effective communication of business information.

OAK TREE PRESS

T: + 353 86 244 1633
E: info@oaktreepress.com
W: www.oaktreepress.com / www.SuccessStore.com.